An insight into depression

An insight into
depression

Chris Ledger and Wendy Bray

CWR
WAVERLEY ABBEY INSIGHT SERIES

Published 2009 by CWR, Waverley Abbey House, Waverley Lane, Farnham, Surrey GU9
8EP, UK. Registered Charity No. 294387. Registered Limited Company No. 1990308.
Reformatted 2019.
The rights of Christine Ledger and Wendy Bray to be identified as the authors of this
work have been asserted by them in accordance with the Copyright, Designs and
Patents Act 1988, sections 77 and 78.
For a list of National Distributors, visit cwr.org.uk/distributors
Unless otherwise indicated, all Scripture references are from the Holy Bible: New
International Version (NIV), copyright © 1973, 1978, 1984 by the International
Bible Society.
Concept development, editing, design and production by CWR.
Printed in the UK by Page Bros.
ISBN: 978-1-78951-237-3

WAVERLEY ABBEY INSIGHT SERIES

The *Waverley Abbey Insight Series* has been developed in response to the great need to help people understand and face some key issues that many of us struggle with today. CWR's ministry spans teaching, training and publishing, and this series draws on all of these areas of ministry.

Sourced from material first presented over Insight Days by CWR, presenters and authors have worked in close co-operation to bring this series together, offering clear insight, teaching and help on a broad range of subjects and issues. Bringing biblical understanding and insight, these books are written both for those who help others and those who face these issues themselves.

Where case studies are included, names and details have been changed to protect the identity of the people concerned. Permission has been given for the stories to be told.

Contents

Foreword by Adrian Plass   8

Introduction   10

1 What is depression?   13

2 Living with depression   31

3 Climbing out of depression – The first steps   51

4 Beginning to climb – Taking practical action   69

5 Continuing the climb – Managing our thinking   91

6 Under the dark cloud – Depression and faith   111

Appendix 1: How depressed am I? Rating my mood   129

Appendix 2: Daily thought diary   131

Further reading   132

Helpful information   134

Endnotes   135

Foreword

Many years ago a stress illness changed my life. I was never confident about the authenticity of my personality, and this explosive, involuntary abdication from most forms of responsibility confirmed my doubts. The situation was complicated by my being an evangelical Christian at a time when depression and breakdown were generally regarded as symptoms of spiritual dysfunction. Some people told my wife that recovery was a matter of identifying how I had 'moved outside the Lord's will' and then simply moving back into it. Bridget gave them short shrift, but not everybody is blessed with such a devoted gatekeeper.

It was a time of confusion, disorientation and creeping dread that the best was past, and the worst was yet to come. However, this appalling experience resulted in personal reconstruction and a brand-new career of speaking and writing. This is wonderful, but those who have cowered in a similar little corner of hell will understand that I shall always feel and think with a limp. I'm glad. We hurt, limping ones identify with imperfection, or to put it another way, with the whole of the rest of the world.

I wish *An Insight into Depression* had been available then. Wendy Bray and Chris Ledger combine warmth and reassurance with practical suggestions and sane biblical insight. What a blessing for those in daily conflict with Winston Churchill's Black Dog of depression, to be offered such a loving, supportive aid to healing. I particularly appreciated the catalogue of suggested practical and personal responses. Jesus says the truth will set us free, and learning the truth that there are no 'oughts', and that sufferers should be kind to themselves will, by the grace of God, fling open doors that might have appeared jammed shut forever.

The list in Chapter 2 of myths that need exploding is equally liberating. The twin convictions that depression is abnormal, and somehow 'my fault' are lodged in the minds of many I speak to. The pall of darkness cast over this subject by ignorance and fear creates a dank and gloomy breeding ground for false perception and nonsense. Chris and Wendy deal effectively with these devilish weeds.

The book's conclusion, that depression need not be ultimately negative, is tough for those going through it, but absolutely essential. Without that distant glow in the darkness it really is difficult to function from day to day. When Solomon had finished building his temple there was great rejoicing in the magnificent new house of God. Suddenly a cloud descended, extinguishing the celebrations. 'Don't worry,' Solomon told the dismayed assembly, 'God told me he would be in the cloud.'

An Insight into Depression confirms that pattern of divine involvement and compassion, meeting minds and hearts in the cloud of emotional pain that obscures us, however impenetrable it may appear, and offering the sweet and eternal possibility of hope.

Adrian Plass

Introduction

Regularly discussed in magazines, on television and the internet, and the subject of many a self-help book, depression is often considered to be a modern condition. However, research suggests that depression has been with us for thousands of years[1] and that many prominent men and women throughout the ages have suffered from it. Some of them, including the likes of Winston Churchill and Virginia Woolf, have written vividly about their experiences.

The term 'depression', when used to describe an emotional experience, is often ill-defined and ill-applied – used to cover everything from a bad day to suicidal misery. As I write, a national newspaper announces that I have just lived through 'the most depressed day of the year'. It was named as such because a number of negative factors had 'collided', including the weather and the economic health of the nation. And only yesterday a friend reported that a neighbour was 'so very depressed again'.

Few have lived a life free from depression, either as sufferers or as the friends or carers of depressed people. Whether we suffer personally or not, depression is an inescapable part of all our lives and, as such, requires understanding. But perhaps true understanding of what it means to be depressed comes less from textbooks, surveys and definitions, and more from the relationships we build: as friends or carers we can learn to understand the challenges depressed people face, the world-views they adopt, and the pathways that have led them to a place of depression. It may be our responsibility – and our privilege – to help them move beyond it.

This book, building on CWR's Insight into Depression teaching day led by Chris Ledger, aims to help us understand depression by reflecting on individual experience, psychological research and professional practice. The book includes personal insight and practical activities for both the sufferer and the helper, and offers a holistic and God-centred approach to understanding and moving beyond depression.

Wendy Bray

When we think of depression, the phrase 'mental health' is often not far away. Factors contributing to mental health may be emotional, social, psychological, physical – and also spiritual. To be 'mentally well' is to be able to continually develop emotionally, socially, psychologically and, we believe, spiritually – even when faced with the difficulties that life throws at us. In other words, having good mental health enables a person to function well in life, developing and sustaining mutually satisfying relationships.

The Mental Health Foundation gives a secular definition of 'spirituality', defining it as 'whatever gives an individual's life meaning, purpose and fulfilment'. Thus it is widely accepted that our spirituality plays a crucial role in mental health, because our religious and spiritual experiences contribute to the shaping of our inner world.

With many years' experience of counselling people suffering from depression, I have learnt much from each unique person as they have struggled to make sense of their suffering and find ways to grow into great wholeness. Having also supported close friends and family members through episodes of debilitating depression, I have seen at first hand the torment and distress that it brings, not only to the sufferer but also – through no fault of their own – to those around them. Depression, however, is not a state of helplessness, although it often feels like this to the sufferer. There are ways in which people can help themselves to climb out of the darkness. The purpose of this book is to present some of those ways.

The stories used to illustrate how sufferers experience depression are not based on anyone in particular. Names and some details have been changed to protect anonymity.

Chris Ledger

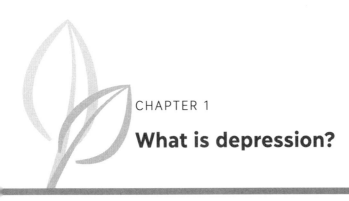

CHAPTER 1

What is depression?

'Depression' is a common word used to describe a geographical or graphical dip, a financial slump, or even a particular type of weather – as well as a person's mood. When life is tough going, flat, below par, seemingly losing its value, or dark and cloudy, we often say we are 'depressed'.

But where our mental health is concerned, defining exactly what we mean by 'depression' is difficult, simply because we are all so different. While general or clinical definitions offer a starting point, true understanding asks that they be just that: a place to begin.

Depression is generally defined as:

- 'An emotional state of dejection and sadness ranging from mild discouragement and downheartedness to feelings of utter hopelessness and despair' (The World Health Organisation);
- 'A pathological state of extreme dejection or melancholy, often with physical symptoms' (*The Oxford Compact English Dictionary*).

Personal definitions may help – or confuse – us further. Inevitably, they will be shaped by individuals' own experiences. Some will refer to depression as 'an illness', others 'an episode'. For some it might be constant and recurring – 'something I live with'; for others, an isolated period – 'the worst time of my life'. For many, depression is best described through metaphor: a black shroud or a black cloud; being stuck in a pit or trapped in a prison.

Winston Churchill suffered from bipolar disorder (formerly known as 'manic-depressive disorder'), a type of depression involving great and unpredictable mood swings from high to low. He described his low times as 'the black dog': a creature that followed him about wherever he went.[1] Psychiatrist Sue Chance writes that Churchill's use of the metaphor 'black dog' speaks volumes: 'The nickname implies both familiarity and an attempt at mastery, because while that dog may sink his fangs into one's person every now and then, he's still, after all, only a dog, and he can be cajoled sometimes and locked up at other times.'[2]

And yet, experts – including those who suffer themselves – are divided over both why depression is so common, and exactly what constitutes a clinical definition. The American novelist and essayist William Styron wrote, 'Depression is a disorder of mood, so mysteriously painful and elusive [as]... to verge close to being beyond description. It thus remains nearly incomprehensible to those who have not experienced it.'[3]

Perhaps, then, it is helpful to consider what depression is *not*.

The incidental, reactive or periodic feeling of sadness or distress which inevitably presents itself in everyday life, should not be confused with what is generally called 'clinical depression' (more later about that). Sadness and distress are totally normal, indeed necessary, human reactions to everyday events. If the weather is continually grey and rainy, we may feel miserable. If a pet dies or a loved one goes away from home for a long time, we will understandably be sad. When one frustrating or disappointing thing after another seems to fill our day, we can feel 'fed up'. Many of us have days when we wake up in a bad mood, or feel low all day. It is common for our moods to go up and down. Sometimes this is due to illness, and women's moods can be affected by their menstrual cycle.

Depression, however, is more complex. It has many faces, and presents itself in different ways according to the individual personality and life-experience of the sufferer. It is, consequently, the *experience* of depression, rather than the general and common signs and symptoms, that can give us the greatest insight and understanding.

So, in terms of our *experience*, we are depressed when:

- life seems meaningless and hopeless;
- we feel an 'emptiness' or 'numbness' that makes us question the point of living;
- we can't see a single thing to look forward to;
- we feel so miserable that we can't motivate ourselves to perform simple tasks, such as washing or eating;
- we feel alone, even in a friendly group of people, as if there is a barrier between ourselves and others;
- we are tearful for long periods, at unexpected moments, or for no apparent reason;
- what is familiar and safe becomes burdensome or threatening.

Although depression often wears the face of fear and anxiety, stress, or an inability to cope, it has nothing to do with lack of courage – the bravest and most capable men and women can be affected. Nor has depression got anything to do with lack of intellect or understanding, since clever and insightful people are often afflicted. In fact, there is a startlingly high incidence of creative, artistic and intellectually brilliant individuals amongst the roll-call of those who have suffered depression –

Charles Darwin and Marie Curie, for example – and many people have given much to society despite their depression.

The biggest handicap to helping depressed people is the concept of depression itself. The view of many professionals – and sufferers – is that 'depression' is too broad and heterogeneous a category to be useful as a basis for effective treatment. This is why continuing debate and new initiatives are needed both to tackle the perceived stigma of depression, and to generate the necessary response. One such initiative is the Time to Change campaign, designed to address mental health discrimination (see time-to-change.org.uk).

So what do we need to know about depression?

How are we to understand depression in the context of our day-to-day lives? *Why* do we get depressed? *What* makes us more vulnerable to depression, and *how* does it affect the life of a Christian? Can we find meaning in the experience?

Research by sociologist George Brown and psychologist Tirril Harris[4] has found that most people did not get depressed because there was something wrong with their personality, but because there was something wrong in their lives. The researchers concluded that, in its first onset, depression usually occurs for a reason – often in the face of a serious difficulty. Most of the serious life events that cause depression are in some way or other connected to loss: the loss of a sense of worth, of an important relationship or role, or of a life-project that has been fundamental to one's identity.

In England, in any given week, around one in six people are

said to experience a common mental health problem such as depression or anxiety. In 2016, figures showed that 3.3 people in 100 were diagnosed with depression. In 2018, 70.9 million prescriptions for antidepressants were given out, almost doubling the 36 million in 2008.[5]

Depression is so widespread that if we asked the right questions, we would discover that one in three people has been diagnosed with a psychiatric disorder in the course of a year – and that the other two may not be telling the truth! Among those aged 15 to 45 it is estimated that depression is by far the biggest cost to the worldwide healthcare budget, second only to that of cancer.

While the epidemic of depression may seem to be largely driven by the drug companies – anti-depressants such as Prozac, Citalopram and Sertraline have become household names – self-diagnosis and labelling have also contributed to the increase. Those who suffer low moods and emotional difficulties are these days likely to say 'I'm depressed', rather than 'I'm facing a difficult situation, that's why I'm feeling down'.

So often, modern media sends the message that life should be perfect. As an affluent and comfortable society – at least in the West – we often find it hard to accept suffering as a normal part of life. Depression in some ways may be the flipside of our reliance on instant solutions and immediate gratification: 'If life doesn't go perfectly, I will be depressed.' But caution is needed here. It is easy for such comments to dismiss the experience of those for whom depression is an intolerable burden, rather than a result of their lifestyle choice. We always need to focus on the person, not the label.

As Christians, we may have an extra factor to tackle when dealing with depression. Many Christians associate depression with sin, pointing to the apostle Paul's call: 'Rejoice in the Lord always!' Being in a church full of people who do not understand depression, and whose simple answer is that we should always be full of joy, will make the depressed Christian feel worse. Their inability to act on this 'helpful suggestion' will cause further isolation and a deepening sense of guilt. We should no more feel ashamed or embarrassed when suffering from depression than we would when suffering from a broken leg. It is OK to struggle, and to learn to accept our human frailty. Depression is biblical: as we will discover in our final chapter, the Bible accepts depression as a natural part of life. If we are depressed, we are in good – and God-cared-for – company.

Depression is not usually caused by our spiritual state, but it will often affect our spiritual life. We might see our depression in spiritual terms, feeling that we have let God down or done something wrong. Those in Christian leadership, Christian counsellors and others may occasionally think the same way and, as John White says, 'may rightly diagnose a spiritual problem in one client but miss a depressive illness in another so that faith is encouraged when faith is impossible, or praise encouraged when the heart is as withered as a prune'.[6] Symptoms may be addressed, but the illness continues.

As fallen individuals, we habitually focus on self rather than God. Depression will invariably lead us to do so to a greater extent. Our eyes may be turned away from God and His perspective to focus more intently on ourselves, our situation and our feelings. Time spent with God in prayer or meditation on the Bible may consequently become difficult, seem pointless, or just take too much effort. When we do pray, our mind can wander easily into misery and misunderstanding. Church activities – corporate worship and being together with other (presumably 'happy') Christians – may be too much to bear, so we may withdraw, removing ourselves from a potential support network.

> Lynne suffered from postnatal depression following the birth of her second child, a boy. She withdrew from all church activities while she was so unhappy, because the effort of caring for a toddler and new baby was enough to cope with: any spare emotional energy she wanted to reserve for her children.
>
> Lynne considered herself under the gaze of other Christians in her church, who she thought were 'judging' her, and she wanted even those who were kind to her to leave her alone. But Lynne's friend Polly did not give up. She called at Lynne's house almost every day. Often Lynne did not answer the door, but slowly she recognised Polly's persistence as real care and concern. On one occasion Polly, who was shorter than Lynne, ducked under the arm that was barring Polly's way into the house! This was just the cheeky, decisive action that Lynne needed. Polly helped her to do a few things around the house, and they chatted as they worked. Gradually, Polly was able to encourage Lynne to go out with her and both their children. Polly took all their children to a parent and toddler group one morning a week so that Lynne had some time to herself. That genuine love and concern began a very special and honest friendship between the two women.

What are the signs and symptoms of depression?

It is helpful to take an experiential and person-centred approach to understanding depression. It is also important to identify some general signs and symptoms, to help us distinguish between clinical depression, which can also be called a depressive illness, and just a 'bad day'.

Signs

The signs and symptoms of depression can be subtle or severe. If the signs go unnoticed for too long, or the sufferer is too apprehensive or ashamed to deal with them, the problem can be compounded. Friends and relatives may be the first to notice that something is wrong, and they may be well placed to encourage a visit to a GP if necessary.

The most common request of a depressed person is someone to talk to. While a man may be less likely to talk a problem through, a woman who has no one to confide in may feel rejected and ignored. As a consequence, she is more likely to get depressed than a woman with a family member or friend she can confide in.[7] Many sufferers feel that whatever 'this' is, they can't deal with it by themselves. Consequently, it is important that the depressed person understands that they are not alone: either in suffering the depression, or in trying to deal with it.

Psychiatrist Martin Seligman describes depression as 'the common cold of psychiatry'.[8] Certainly an episode of depression can be slight and short-lived, perhaps in reaction to a distressing event; at the other end of the spectrum, however, it can cause emotional, and even physical, paralysis. Our coping abilities will determine how we survive it, and whether it leaves us with guilt or long-term damage.

Despite the widespread incidence of depression and the extensive research into it, little is known about its cause. Dr Grace Ketterman suggests a group of intermingling influences[9]:

1. Genetic predisposition
2. Family practices and beliefs
3. Impact of the environment
4. Stress

We know that depression is a 'brain state', like happiness. When everyday life becomes stressful and things become 'too much', the working of our brain is affected to the extent that a 'shutdown' trigger is activated, which says 'Enough!' The trigger may be pulled for various reasons. In particular, we are more likely to shut down when we are too demanding or critical of ourselves. When depressed, we often focus on feelings of pain, emptiness and pointlessness. We make negative judgments and criticise ourselves, pointing out what we think are our own mistakes and inadequacies. Negative self-talk begins in earnest: in fact, we may bully ourselves. A toxic thought-life may not always cause depression but will certainly maintain it, because every thought has a corresponding electrochemical reaction in our brain. Thus, negative thoughts release chemicals that have a negative effect on the working of our bodies.

Depressed moods magnify the negative thoughts and focus on them, intensifying the pain and beginning a vicious downward spiral of negativity. Living with depression means learning to bring balance to our thoughts and feelings. If this can be done at an early stage, as soon as we recognise signs and symptoms, then the first vital steps can be made in climbing out of the depression. The longer we spend falling downwards, the harder it will be to regain balance and come back to the surface again.

We have already mentioned that it is normal – indeed part of being human – for us to feel up or down at different times. But we may go beyond these normal feelings, and a doctor may diagnose 'clinical depression'.

What is clinical depression?

The term simply refers to an experience of depression that would be recognised and treated by a professional practitioner, perhaps a GP, according to a guide such as *The Diagnostic and Statistical Manual of Mental Disorders*.[10] This is one of the standard guides used by psychologists and psychiatrists to distinguish between normal and abnormal states. Symptoms like these may be evident:

1. *Depressed mood*: Feeling sad, low, hopeless or irritable for long periods. Often remarking on a numbness or emptiness. Possible extreme, even violent, mood swings. Tearfulness. Such moods may be expressed as: 'Everything seems so pointless: what am I living for?'

2. *Loss of pleasure or interest in usual activities*: Nothing seems enjoyable or fun any more. Motivation to engage in usual interests and activities is very low: 'I can't be bothered: it's all too much effort.'

3. *Significant weight change*: This may be gain or loss, with either 'comfort eating' or loss of appetite: 'I can't stop eating' or 'I just ate a biscuit for my meals today'.

4. *Sleep disturbances*: Insomnia, with difficulty in getting to sleep or early morning waking; 'I lay awake all night thinking

– 3am is the worst time for me;' 'hypersomnia': 'I hide under the duvet and sleep, because this blots out the pain'.

5. *Changes in level of activity*: Either a marked slowness in speaking and doing things, or increased agitation. Change of activity can cause a swing between the two.

6. *Decreased energy*: Lethargy; fatigue; loss of energy leading to a reduction or loss of motivation: 'I'd rather just sit here all day.'

7. *Loss of confidence and self-esteem*: Feelings of worthlessness with loss of confidence and self-esteem. Feelings of excessive or irrational guilt; hopelessness: 'There's no point in trying because things will never get better.'

8. *Poor concentration and difficulty in thinking*: Difficulty in concentrating, making decisions, thinking rationally or maintaining short-term memory. It becomes easier – and often habitual – to remember bad things rather than good things: 'I don't know who visited today... did anyone? But I remember it rained in the morning.'

9. *Suicidal thoughts or behaviour*: Recurrent thoughts of death or suicide. These may range from fleeting thoughts to real intention – making active plans for suicide: 'What's the point of going on? I don't want to live like this anymore.' (If suicidal thoughts are frequent, it's important to contact a GP as soon as possible. See 'Suicide', on page 27.)

A diagnosis of depression will be made when
- symptoms are present every day, or almost every day, for two weeks, affecting the person's ability to function normally;
- at least one of the first two symptoms in the list above is present.

The health professional will assume that
- four symptoms indicate mild depression;
- six symptoms indicate moderate depression;
- eight symptoms indicate severe depression.

It is also recognised that
- hallucinations or delusions may be present in severe cases.

If these standardised criteria are met, depression will usually be diagnosed as clinical. Awareness of, and prompt response to symptoms, is essential.

This clear framework not only assists the diagnosis of clinical depression, but enables an understanding of what *isn't* clinical depression.

A useful website is The Charlie Waller Memorial Trust, where you can find 'Depression – the warning signs' (cwmt.org.uk). Different types of clinical depression can be described as follows:

- *Major depression*: when intense bouts last for weeks at a time.
- *Lingering depression*: which remains present at a low level for years.
- *Reactive depression*: an 'adjustment disorder' during or after a specific and traumatic life experience such as bereavement. Adjustment may be complicated and slower than expected, causing problems with daily functioning.
- *Bipolar affective disorder*: includes periods of elation and hyperactivity. Formerly known as manic-depressive disorder, this affects one in ten sufferers and may be hereditary.

It is also helpful to consider how signs and symptoms are presented in our *experience* of depression. Symptoms fall into five main areas:

Physical symptoms

We may experience:
- Changes in sleep patterns, appetite, weight and energy level.
- Loss of energy; physical pain, eg headache, backache, gastrointestinal disturbances and decreased sexual desire. Women may suffer menstrual cycle irregularities.

Emotional symptoms

We may experience:
- Low mood with feelings of sadness, hopelessness, pessimism and despair; anxiety and fear; anger and resentment, guilt, a sense of worthlessness, helplessness and failure.
- Negative feelings towards others and towards oneself.
- Loss of desire to live, with inability to be comforted.
- Loss of sense of humour and difficulty in laughing.
- Feeling emotionally 'flat'; a 'don't-care' attitude. Persistent sad or empty mood; tearfulness.
- Feelings of dread.
- Feelings of guilt.

Mental (thinking) symptoms

We may experience:
- The tendency to view ourselves, the world and the future through a negative lens: our thinking becomes unbalanced. When life seems cruel or unfair we may say to ourselves: 'If only I had...'; 'If only I hadn't...'; 'If only it was...'; 'If only it wasn't...'; 'I should...'; 'I ought...' We may become self-critical:

'It's my fault'; 'I'm inadequate'; 'I'm a bad person.' We judge ourselves to be too fat, too disorganised, and so on, and begin to criticise ourselves. We may judge ourselves very harshly.
- Anxious thoughts.
- A tendency to interpret events in a very negative way, seeing ourself, life and the future as bleak and unchangeable. We feel our life is meaningless, hopeless and purposeless.
- Self-introspection: our attention is turned inward.
- Difficulty in concentrating, poor memory, and inability to make even simple decisions.

Behavioural symptoms

We may experience:
- Withdrawal from social scenes. (We retreat into a 'prison' or 'cave'.) Avoidance of other people.
- Sad personal appearance and use of sad words.
- A loss of interest in personal appearance.
- Restlessness. We may become agitated as opposed to lethargic.
- A loss of interest in, or care about, our usual responsibilities.
- Reduced activity, and loss of enjoyment in recreation. We stop doing the things we have generally enjoyed (eg reading, sports, hobbies, playing with children, listening to music). This eliminates rewarding experiences, perpetuating the sense of the worthlessness of life.
- A 'shrinking world'. As we become more inwardly focused, we shut down and 'shrink' our world.

Spiritual symptoms

We may experience:

- The belief that God is distant or has deserted us just when we need Him most: 'I can't pray.'
- A sense of failure or guilt.
- The belief that God is an angry monster or cruel alien who is laughing at us.
- A desire to bargain with God.
- A sense of being rejected by God.
- A belief that salvation, or faith in God, is lost or has been removed.
- A tendency to be disturbed by thoughts of God.
- Difficulty in engaging in spiritual activities: prayer, reading, Bible study, fellowship and worship.

Suicide

At its most extreme, depression can lead the sufferer to contemplate escaping their emptiness or torment by ending their life. Suicidal thoughts and attempts are, perhaps shockingly, prevalent in our society: half the population will have suicidal feelings of moderate to severe levels, at some point in their lives.

Whatever the cause or level of despair that we, or those we are supporting, reach in depression, it is clear that time should not be lost in referring those who suffer thoughts of suicide for professional medical or psychiatric help.

Activity

Use the 'How depressed am I?' exercise in Appendix 1 to record how you, or someone you are helping, is experiencing depression.

Don't expect too much analysis at this stage, but use the activity simply to give the experience some shape and 'place'.

Reflection

For use alone, with a carer/friend, or as a carer/friend alongside one who is depressed.

Archbishop Rowan Williams writes that prayer is 'getting ourselves into the light of His presence, putting aside our defences and disguises, coming into silence and stillness so that what stands before God is not the performer, the mask, the habits of self-promotion and self-protection, but the naked me'.[11]

It may be difficult to understand that it is our honesty, and our spiritual and emotional nakedness, that constitute true prayer. But if we are to welcome God at the point where He can reach us and heal us, we can hold nothing back from Him. Neither can we hide: for to hide would be to hide from His love, and deprive ourselves of it.

- Imagine yourself taking tentative steps into the loving presence of God.
- Tell Him – and you may find it easier to write, or perhaps draw – exactly how you are feeling now. Hold nothing back.

    Your words need not be eloquent; your drawing need not be fine art. You may not even be able to use words or symbols: sighs and tears are also heard by God, and are precious to Him.

- Be brave enough to allow yourself to be emotionally and spiritually 'naked' before God. You may find it easier to do so just for a few seconds or minutes at first, and build up day by day: God will wait.
- At the end of each time, ask Him to hold and protect you, assuring you of His love as you embark on the difficult climb out of depression.

Prayer

Lord God, there is no darkness in You. Yet the mystery is that You are also the God of 'dazzling darkness'.[12] Through the experience of Your Son Jesus, You know what it is to suffer in a dark place. Make me brave enough to reach out and take the hand that is offered in the darkness – and find it to be Yours. Stand with me now as we search for even a pinprick of light offered by You in this place of depression. Guide me towards it, Lord. May Your light grow clearer and brighter in the days ahead.
Amen.

CHAPTER 2

Living with depression

Who gets depressed?

Depression is widespread across all ages, cultures and backgrounds, and amongst men, women and children. Four per cent of young people become seriously depressed in the UK each year.[1]

Women are more likely to ask for medical help with depression. This doesn't mean men are less likely to become depressed, but they are less likely to recognise their symptoms. Men may also use different coping strategies. Their symptoms are more likely to be outward: slow movement and speech, hostility, and alcohol abuse.[2] Some psychiatrists have described men's depression as a 'big build' of debilitating destructive behaviours, which start with numbing and avoidance, then lead to violence to oneself and others.[3]

Women often experience episodes of depression which are linked to their childbearing function. These may include post-natal depression, menstrual and menopausal depression, and depression linked to the loss of grown-up children who leave the family home, commonly called 'empty nest syndrome'. It is a mistake to consider these depressive episodes as 'merely' hormonal. While some can be traced to hormone imbalance or disorder, far more depressive episodes have an emotional basis linked to loss, fear, a connection with a negative early life experience, or a sense of having passed beyond the time of usefulness as a woman.

Fiona waved her first daughter off to university with joy. When the time came for her second – and youngest – child to make a similar move two years later, Fiona was equally delighted. She also looked forward to some time to herself, and the opportunity to reconnect with her husband at the beginning of a new stage of their lives. At first Fiona busied herself with activities that she had planned in advance, and Christmas was full of joy, welcoming the two girls home. But by February Fiona was very low. Often tearful, she found herself looking through old photograph albums and weeping at the way the years had seemingly passed so quickly. The house seemed so empty.

Fiona told no one just how low she was feeling, thinking that people would say she was 'being silly'.

Fiona's husband then went away on business, deepening her sense of isolation. It was only when she found herself sleeping in her daughter's bed, clutching her daughter's beloved but abandoned toy rabbit and sobbing, that Fiona realised that she was very depressed. She confided in a friend who had recently struggled with her own son's departure to university and, to her relief, found that she too had kept much of her sadness to herself. Both women encouraged each other to understand that their feelings were of grief and loss, and that they were not 'being silly' at all. They began to work together to handle this new and difficult phase of life, and started an informal coffee evening for parents in a similar position. Organising these events gave Fiona a new sense of purpose and she began to feel a little better. She still missed her daughters terribly – although she never told them just how much! But she began to gain some perspective on her situation, and her depression slowly lifted.

Exploding the myths about depression

When we first begin to experience a depressive episode, our self-dialogue often betrays how we feel about the state of being depressed, and this 'inner conversation' can offer some insight into the origin of the depression itself. In order to move forward through our depression, we may need to address the inaccurate, unhelpful or misleading beliefs that our self-talk discloses.

Myth number one:
'Depression is abnormal.'

Truth
The literal meaning of 'abnormal' is 'out of the ordinary'. But research shows that depression is common, or ordinary. To call depression 'abnormal' is like calling the common cold a bizarre occurrence. Rather, depression is a common and universal signal that something in our life is not working well. Instead of looking inside ourselves with blame and reproach, we may need to look outward, with a genuine desire to find out what isn't working in the way we are living our life.

Myth number two:

'Much worse things happen to other people and they cope without getting depressed. I'm just weak and stupid – I should be able to cope.'

Truth

We are not 'weak and stupid' just because we think we are unable to cope. Such feelings of helplessness are symptoms of depression, and are not a sign that we are inferior to anyone else. In addition, when depressed our tendency is to focus on people who are getting on with life. We tend not to notice those who are struggling.

There are times when depression becomes much more obviously like an illness than simply 'not coping'. That can happen to the most determined, capable and successful of people. It is not a sign of weakness but of a breaking-point, or a sign of being off-balance. What is needed is help to move beyond that breaking-point, and to regain some balance.

Myth number three:

'There's no reason why I should be depressed, because nothing bad or traumatic has happened to me. It must be my fault.'

Truth

This myth comes from an assumption that all depression is 'reactive' – occurring as a result of a distressing event. But sometimes it is difficult to understand why we have become depressed. It's easy to look inwards and think we are to blame. That isn't true. With help, we may be able to see why we are vulnerable to depression at a particular point in our lives. If some recognition and understanding can be reached, we can release ourselves from blame and guilt and move forward.

Myth number four:

'I should be able to cope by myself and get on with life. I shouldn't need help. I don't think talking to anyone is helpful – it's self-indulgent.'

Truth

'Should' is a loaded word, full of demands and unfair expectations. There is no rule that says 'You *should* be able to cope'. These words betray a sense of guilt and encourage a tendency to shut oneself away from others, when often what helps the depressed person is to share fears and feelings honestly. We can't 'snap out of' depression, whereas talking about ourselves with others in a constructive way often proves to be very helpful.

Myth number five:

'I've always felt like this. Why is it being labelled as depression?'

Truth

Some of us may consider that we have felt unhappy since childhood, to the extent that we have got used to feeling very low. We believe that such feelings are part of our inbuilt character or personality rather than the result of long-term depression. It can be a revelation when, with skilled help, the long-term depressed person discovers 'I don't have to feel like this – it isn't me.'

Myth number six:

'Depression is all biological, therefore only anti-depressants can make my brain right.'

Truth

It's true that medication can help. But scientific evidence does not support defining depression as a biological disease, and depression is not recognised as such by the World Health Organisation. Depression can be understood as a disturbance of brain metabolism, but it is not independent of life circumstances. Sometimes, depression is caused by unhelpful ways of trying to make sense of hurts and problems. Perhaps this is why some people come through traumatic and painful events scarred but well, while others remain damaged and get depressed. Our recovery from such events – and from the depression they may lead to – is helped by changing the way we think and behave.

Myth number seven:

'I'm a failure if I take "happy pills". Christians ought not to be depressed.'

Truth

It's not true that we have failed if we take medication for depression, any more than if we take painkillers for a headache. Christians are as vulnerable as anyone else. And faith does not exclude the kind of trauma or life event that may lead to reactive depression – or any other kind of depression. Just as some people are vulnerable to a physical illness such as diabetes, and need to take medication or administer insulin, some of us are more vulnerable to depression and will also need to take medication in the form of anti-depressants. (And by the way, 'ought' is the sister of 'should' and 'shouldn't'!)

Myth number eight:

'Medication won't help. It can't change the things that are making me depressed.'

Truth

It's true that medication will not change the circumstances with which we are having difficulty, or take away our problems. But appropriate medication does help us to feel better, and enable us to cope with our difficulties in a more clear-headed and effective way. Medication can give us the kind of 'coping spectacles' we need until our own clear vision returns.

Myth number nine:

'Depression is something I "have".'

Truth

We often talk about 'having' depression in the same way that we talk about 'having' a headache. It's as if it has descended on us out of the blue. Are we inevitable victims of depression? Or do we 'bring it on ourselves' – in the same way that drinking too much may bring on a hangover?

Firstly, people who develop depression often begin by having thoughts and doing things that feed the roots of depression – long before they develop the mood-symptoms of depression itself. Their chosen coping mechanisms often cause a long-term depressive effect, even if these seem like the right mechanisms to adopt at the time. So although people may not consciously choose to behave in ways that will cause depression, they may inadvertently sow the seeds.

Secondly, if depression is seen as 'something I have' it can encourage us to live in a state of negative acceptance which leads us into a role of 'learned helplessness', of being sick: 'I can't help it – it's just the way I am.' When we are sick, we often wait for something to change rather than proactively working for change ourselves. But depression is like a physical illness in that it has physical and psychological symptoms from which we *can* recover.

Dan grew up as the apple of his parents' eye. Everything Dan wanted, Dan got. A football injury at age twelve began a cycle of attention-seeking behaviour that led to Dan's increased dependency on the 'sympathy' of his parents. They first assumed that Dan had ME and then that he was 'depressed', while doctors found no real symptoms to diagnose either problem. Dan often chose to 'be ill' when his parents wanted to go out or when relatives visited, to the point that they were unable to go out alone together or invite friends or wider family to the house for fear of Dan's often violent reaction. Dan tried university and a part-time job but never coped for long, usually leaving after creating a scene. On other days he would be 'well' and would go shopping for clothes alone, or enjoy a cinema or theatre visit.

Although doctors doubted that there was anything wrong, Dan's parents – and Dan – were by this point caught up in his 'illness': this was a state of 'learned helplessness' for all of them. His parents had been not just sympathetic, but indulgent – but they couldn't admit it. The situation became so difficult that Dan's younger sister (who had graduated from university) refused to stay at home for more than a day, as her brother made her life unbearable. By the time Dan reached the age of thirty

the whole wider family could see what was happening,
but were powerless to help. Dan was stuck in a deep pit
of depression.

What makes us more vulnerable to depression?

Why do some people suffer periodic depression throughout their lives, while others never experience it? Can we 'depression-proof' ourselves, and should we even try? Are we all potentially depressive, or is there a 'depressive type'?

There is no simple answer. Some people are able to say why they are depressed; others find no obvious cause. Some reflection may reveal a confusion of past and present events, or a complex interpretation of life's twists and turns; some 'explanations' make no sense at all to an onlooker. We can, however, find some factors and patterns in life which might help us to understand why some people are more vulnerable to going through periods of depression.

Childhood

As children we often misinterpret what we hear, and become confused by the life going on around us. Even if our childhood wasn't particularly traumatic, we may carry scars into adult life, the result of mixed messages, unspoken expectations or incomplete understanding.

We may have lived in a family that sent negative messages – 'You're stupid'; 'Be good and stay quiet, then we'll love you'; or 'We never wanted you'. Our parents may have been there in person but absent emotionally, or abusive sexually, verbally, physically or emotionally. Our response to such childhood circumstances will be complex. In the absence of any positive messages or a sense of redeeming love, we may believe that the harsh words are true and the painful treatment is deserved. We assume that our parents know what is right and wrong: they are our first frame of reference for understanding the world. So we will act as if the negative messages (words spoken and unspoken) are true. We will define our identity as we grow up, believing that we really are 'stupid', we need to be good in order to be loved, or we are unwanted. Such beliefs, and the feelings that result, can feed life-long depression.

Personality

Is depression hereditary? It seems that any child who grows up with at least one depressed parent might well develop a depressed view of life, and there appear to be some families where depression is part of the generational history. But it is unclear whether these results stem from 'nature' (they are born that way) or 'nurture' (they become that way through circumstances – witnessing a depressed parent).

Apart from family influence, our personalities may be more vulnerable to depression when:
- Our self-esteem is based on achieving success rather than on our sense of worth in our parents' eyes, and in God's eyes.
- We have a 'critical self', a silent observer who criticises us severely but silently.
- We have become entrenched in negative thinking.
- We are non-assertive or frightened of expressing our needs, thoughts and feelings.
- We can't manage or reduce unnecessary stress.

As mentioned earlier, there is considerable evidence that some artistic and creative people suffer depression more often and more severely that those with a logical or scientific type of personality. Any list of 'famous' depressives will be heavily weighted towards artists, writers, actors and musicians. For example, actor and polymath Stephen Fry has helpfully shared his experience of depression. Some creative people insist that their best work – music, writing or visual art – emerges from their periods of depression.

Other sufferers say that they are a 'better person' beyond depression, and that such a period helps them to cope with life better in the long run. Psychiatrist Dr Paul Keedwell of The Institute of Psychiatry in London says, in his interestingly titled book *How Sadness Survived,* that 'essentially depression can give us new and quite radical insights – it can give us a way of responding effectively to challenges we have in life'.[4]

Sensitivity

Having a sensitive character, or a spirit which readily responds to the needs of others, is a wonderful gift. But the flipside of that gift is that we are vulnerable to the thoughtlessness, rudeness, spite and bad temper of others. It isn't enough to 'toughen up' or 'develop a thicker skin'. Criticism can hurt – and hurt deeply. We may feel trampled on, wounded and rejected. If that hurt remains, unhealed and barely hidden, or if it is inadvertently touched upon, it can lead to depression.

If we are sensitive, we might also be particularly vulnerable to:

- *Guilt*: feeling responsible for everything and everyone – regardless of the situation. False guilt can be just as heavy a burden as real guilt.

- *Anger:* having never learnt how to express anger, we suppress it. Myra Chave Jones[5] describes depression as 'frozen rage'. Depression can often be anger internalised. Our bodies try hard to contain it, but can't: depression is often the result.

The Church is sadly full of loving, generous yet hurting people who, in offering themselves in service or in the care of others, have also opened themselves up to pain and rejection. It is ironic that, so often, we find ourselves wounded and alone in the very place that should offer us most love and acceptance: the Church, the body of Christ, who is Himself the 'wounded healer'. There is much loving work to be done in restoring to wholeness those who find themselves in a place of depression for such reasons.

Lack of social support

Pop duo Simon and Garfunkel famously sang of being 'a rock' and 'an island' – but few of us benefit from living alone long-term. Without a familiar social network, we are more inclined to become depressed.

Elderly people, especially those who are housebound or have limited mobility, will be particularly vulnerable to such social isolation and the resulting depression.

Into this 'lonely' category will also fall home workers, long-distance drivers, young mums without transport or friends and family nearby, and those living where their own language is not spoken widely. Wendy reports that one of the most common remarks made by the asylum-seekers in a local support group is 'I'm lonely'. Many such people end their own lives. The inability to communicate our loneliness leads to isolation, depression, and even suicide.

We need each other: we are designed to live in community. We need to talk, be heard, share our feelings and be part of something bigger than ourselves, in order to be fully human.

Life events involving loss

Grief and bereavement bring with them emptiness, numbness, and often a sense that life is pointless. These are completely normal reactions, which generally pass with time: reactive depression often follows bereavement. But such depression can be compounded by other emotional issues: unfinished business within the family; anger; unforgiveness; or a sense of guilt or betrayal.

On closer examination, we usually find that most losses involve more than one kind of bereavement, and a later loss often brings back memories of an earlier one – complicating the problem, and often leading to depression. Counsellors who work with those suffering complicated grief sometimes find that bereavement in adult life connects the sufferer with an unresolved loss in childhood. Sometimes, such grief has become tangled with numerous other losses, making grief overwhelming and possibly leading to deep depression.

Bereavement can mean not just the end of a relationship, but the loss of a sense of usefulness, partnership or purpose (as it did for Fiona earlier in this chapter), as well as a loss of self-confidence. Loss of a job or significant role may lead to a second or subsequent loss – of self-esteem, or a sense of significance. The loss of a home may also involve a loss of security or personal history.

Body chemistry

There is a strong link between body chemistry and moods. Flu and other viruses can leave us feeling miserable and battling

43

with low moods for a considerable time after the illness, as can chemical changes brought about by medication such as antibiotics. Caffeine and alcohol also have a temporary mood-enhancing effect, but both 'set us up for a fall' where mood change is concerned: short-term euphoria may be followed by an emotional slump. Some of us may suffer from Seasonal Affective Disorder (SAD) during the winter months when there is less, or darker, daylight.

Changes in hormone levels during a woman's monthly menstrual cycle, after childbirth, or during menopause, all contribute to mood swings. These may be mild and recognisable 'ups and downs', or violent changes in mood and behaviour that disturb not only the sufferer but those around them.

Postnatal depression

It's important to be reminded, however, that hormones are not the only reason for depression after childbirth. The arrival of a child – even an adopted child – is a hugely life-changing event. However prepared we think we are emotionally, the demands of a new role as parent can be overwhelming. However joyful the birth of a child, the first months of parenting can bring to the surface issues that have been hidden in our emotional baggage for some time: events that happened as we were parented; deep-seated fears about the responsibility of caring for a child; or a sense of losing a former role. This is particularly common with mothers who did a paid job at a responsible, professional level before the birth of their child.

A sense of inadequacy can trigger deep and prolonged postnatal depression, and there may even be a risk of a mother harming her child and/or herself. It is essential that professionals and carers identify the difference between the 'normal' three or four days of 'post-partum blues', and the onset of clinical depression. This more serious depression may not even become apparent until the child is several months old, making it harder to recognise.

Burnout

Prolonged periods of sustained work or pressure will sometimes lead to physical and emotional 'burnout': we may 'burn up' our resources to such a degree that we are left unable to function normally, becoming depressed as a result. Burnout can happen to anyone, from a busy executive balancing too many schedules and deadlines to a young single mum struggling to care for her family and hold down a paid job. Often, we need to come to the realisation that we are human, not superhuman, and that there are limits to our physical and mental energy.

Anxiety

For most of us, anxiety is an occasional part of everyday life: we run to catch a train, or worry about a relative who is facing medical tests. Once an event is past or a situation is resolved, our anxiety usually subsides. But for some of us, worry becomes the 'default setting' for our mind. We worry, full stop. Every thought or activity leads to an anxious state until anxiety is a constant and immovable companion who we would like to get rid of, but who never seems to leave us alone. Our demeanour is marked by a furrowed brow, a wringing of hands, and anxious muttering of 'But what if...?' Worry or fear can be crippling, even paralysing. When anxiety becomes entrenched in our thinking and we are held in its grip it can cause major depression.

Societal causes

Depression is often called a 'modern disease', and our own society with its manifold demands may be seen as the cause of depressive episodes. Oliver James refers to the pressures of 'consumer capitalism'. He says that a capitalist, consumer-focused society like ours encourages us to be independent and individualist, rather than co-dependent and community-oriented: 'We speak much of our personal and individual "rights" rather than our responsibilities to one another. We are encouraged to live according to "having" values: possessing, achieving, wanting, living for the experience and in "must have", "must do" rather than "being" mode: "being, accepting, cherishing, living in the present".'[6]

This contemporary shift in focus and life goals has inevitably led us to believe that life should always be comfortable and perfect, that everything should always go our way, and that we should be living a 'designer life' free from pain and inconvenience. The promotion of enviable 'lifestyles' via film, TV and other forms of media affirms this utopian fantasy. However, it is no secret that those who appear to 'have it all' are not exempt from illness or unhappiness. Indeed, they often experience an emptiness which contradicts their apparent success and celebrity. The impact of changes in the economic climate could challenge the long-held assumption that material wealth makes for a happy life, and could lead us back to values based on 'being' rather than 'having'.

Whatever the origin of depression, most of us do not want to live with it: recognising this is the first step to leaving depression behind.

Activity

The following activity is best done with a friend/carer or skilled listener who can support and encourage the depressed person.

Draw a horizontal 'timeline' of your life, or help the person you are supporting to do so. Identify key life events – births, deaths, marriage, relocation, illness, and so on – up to the present time. Write or draw the mainly 'positive' events above the line, and the more 'negative' events below.

- Can you identify those 'places' in which you were vulnerable to depression?
- Without jumping to conclusions or placing blame, can you identify any 'trigger' events that may have caused a reactive depression?

Now that you have clarified events and facts, turn your timeline into a written or spoken 'story' in which you pay attention to your feelings. Be aware of those feelings that are difficult to name or express, and any names which prompt strong emotions.

Write down these feelings or names if necessary, or mark them on your timeline.

Keep this work somewhere safe and private for future reference. (Chapter 3 particularly addresses the handling of emotions.)

At the end of the activity, remind yourself that these events and feelings are in the past; that God heals our memories and our hurts, and that He can use our honesty before Him to lift us out of a place of depression, whatever – and whoever – has brought us to that place.

If possible, pray together for God's peace, perhaps using the following reflection.

Reflection

Spend some time reflecting on Paul's words from Philippians:

> Do not be anxious about anything, but in everything, by prayer and petition, with thanksgiving, present your requests to God. And the peace of God, which transcends all understanding, will guard your hearts and your minds in Christ Jesus.
>
> Finally, brothers, whatever is true, whatever is noble, whatever is right, whatever is pure, whatever is lovely, whatever is admirable – if anything is excellent or praiseworthy – think about such things. Whatever you have learned or received or heard from me, or seen in me – put it into practice. And the God of peace will be with you.
>
> (Phil. 4:6–9)

Paul tells us to pray first, in the assurance that God will guard our hearts and minds.

Then he tells us to allow our minds to dwell only on what is noble, right, lovely, excellent and praiseworthy.

Lastly, he tells us to get going, and to 'put into practice' all he has taught: right prayer, right thoughts and right actions.

Whatever happens and however we feel, these three priorities, applied consistently, will help us to know that 'the God of peace' is with us.

─────

Prayer

God of peace,

Surveying my life and emotions has been hard and painful work. I may yet need to address anger or hurt, and to give or receive forgiveness; my work may not be over. But I ask that You will take this 'story' of my life for healing; that You will remind me that You have a plan for me: a plan shaped by Your love and tenderness.

Help me to move on from this point in my life: to begin to climb out of the depression that holds me back from the fulfilment of Your plan for me.

Make me brave, Lord; keep my mind on all that is noble, right, lovely, excellent and praiseworthy; and give me Your peace. Amen.

CHAPTER 3

Climbing out of depression – The first steps

Before we consider what might help us find a way out of the depths of depression, it is important to examine why it is so difficult to gather the resources we need to begin the climb 'back to the surface'.

Climbing is hard work. The hardest – and most rewarding – climbs take planning, effort, skill, a lot of nerve, and the support of companions and guides. The climb out of the dark pit of depression is no different.

This chapter focuses on preparing to climb, and the first footholds. It aims to help us understand what makes it difficult to even *begin* climbing; to recognise how we function as human beings, and how we can deal with the painful emotions that weigh us down and make climbing so difficult when we have hardly started. The chapter then goes on to suggest some very practical steps to help us make progress.

What might stop us from beginning the climb?

Too often, we try to climb with so much baggage weighing us down that before we've gone very far we are breathless, exhausted and unable to continue. We find ourselves stuck on a ledge, and the only way seems to be back down again.

Alternatively, although the emotional 'baggage' we carry

may be heavy, we have become comfortable with it. Yet examining our baggage and deciding whether we can leave it behind is fundamental to making progress. Our baggage often includes:

Bag 1: High standards
– 'I'll never be good enough'
We often find it difficult to accept that our best is good enough, as we may demand perfection of ourselves. When we fail to reach our self-imposed – and often unrealistic – goals, we blame ourselves. Similarly, if other people and the world at large don't live up to our expectations, we struggle to cope, finding it difficult to settle for less than perfection (see *Insight into Perfectionism*)[1].

We show an inability to let things be and a tendency to be over-critical; we are resentful and unforgiving when our expectations and standards are not met. Jung described such behaviour as 'the well-known bad moods and irritability of the over-virtuous'.[2] Perfectionism, packed tightly (and perfectly!) into our bag, can make it difficult for us to climb out of depression.

Bag 2: Fear of rejection
– 'They won't want me anyway'
Some of us who become depressed will have experienced a great deal of rejection and bullying in our lives. We will consequently fear exposure, and will not want to lift our head above the parapet – let alone the surface. We fear the familiar flying arrows of rejection that have often pierced our heart. Those arrows may have wounded us in early childhood as we were teased, victimised or abused. We could only make sense

of the experience by saying: 'I was a bad child. I deserved to be rejected.' Nevertheless, fear of the arrows of painful rejection will go on into adult life. 'If only someone would pull out those arrows,' we think, 'then the pain will ease.' But if nobody does, over time that pain changes into a dull, heavy ache. That fear of rejection keeps us in the pit of depression because it is just too risky to climb up into the world. Any climb can only be attempted in a cowed and fearful position. Our self-esteem needs restoration so that we can lift our head above the surface.

Bag 3: Protection against disappointment
– 'Expect the worst'
For the 'expect the worst' climbers amongst us, pessimism is habitual. We are always looking on the dark side, and are deterred by every pitfall that faces us. We may never feel joyful, but at least life is miserably predictable! Pessimism can become such a part of our character that we find comfort and security in our suffering, and in the belief that our convictions of the worst-case scenario have been confirmed: 'Of course, I expected it – that kind of thing always happens to me.' The pessimists amongst us will expect our feet to slip as we climb, or expect to be buried beneath a landfall. Even if we do get to the surface, it will undoubtedly be raining. We need to shed the wet-weather gear and first-aid kit we carry, and understand that optimism cuts down our weight as we climb. (Some of the 'renewed thinking' exercises in the next chapter may help us here.)

Bag 4: The martyr's burdens
– 'My problems are bigger than anyone else's'
As the martyrs amongst us get ready to climb, we are muttering: 'No one can feel as bad as me... my problems are so much worse';

'Why am I the only one in my family to suffer like this?' In fact, we martyrs will probably have thrown a pity party in our hole of depression. But we are in that hole because we have made the assumption that everybody else's lives are perfect – when that is far from the truth. 'When we are entranced by our own suffering,' says Dorothy Rowe, 'we become oblivious to the suffering around us.'[3]

We can become a different kind of martyr when, in acknowledging the suffering of others, we become convinced that we are the only person who can help. We may even collect other people's burdens in order to feel good, taking pride in our status as helper because we need to feel needed. But that role can overburden us, and tip us into depression ourselves: 'I can't tell him this or that… because if I do I'll upset him.' The martyrs among us need to climb with others, acknowledging a balance between our own concerns and our responsibility to fellow climbers.

Bag 5: Suffering is a friend
– 'I suffer, therefore I am'

Sometimes our suffering becomes a 'learned behaviour' which we use to give ourselves significance: 'If I suffer and let everyone know I'm low, then I'm noticed and my life has some significance.'

As Christians, we recognise that the symbol of Christianity is the image of the cross and Christ's death – bleeding, wounded, pierced and broken. As a result, some Christians see suffering as a very important part of their Christian walk. They believe that through self-sacrifice and suffering they attain salvation. They dismiss the clear Christian message to love others as we love ourselves, and the promise that Jesus came to give us abundant – rather than agonising – life. Some of us have never given ourselves permission to enjoy life to the full as God intended. When we see our life as a tragedy we feel significant, indeed omnipotent, in our suffering. But that sense of significance and omnipotence can bury us in depression.

The suffering climbers among us need to know that God is the source of the sunshine we can see above the surface *and* the grit beneath our feet. We may need to be helped to understand the abundance and lavish (1 John 3:1) nature of God's love for us as we climb.

Bag 6: Fear of falling apart if pain is faced
– 'I can't look!'
If it feels too painful to process the traumatic experiences of our past, we prefer to live on painkillers rather than stop the pain at source. If our wound is obvious, we choose to constantly reapply a sticking plaster. Yet living with the pain and the wound may lead to long-term – even lifelong – depression that will remain while the wound remains untreated.

Those climbers among us with obvious wounds need support, and the climb may be a slow one. It may even be worse than the pit for a while. It is not so much that baggage needs to be left behind, but that healing is needed on the way. We may need a companion in our place of pain. But perhaps our greatest need is to know that there is healing for the wound and peace beyond the pain, and that both can be attained.

Bag 7: The voluntary prisoner
– 'It's safe in this hole'
Just as a prisoner who has lived in confinement for years has panic attacks in the outside world, those who are depressed can find it frightening to leave the hole of depression in order to start

climbing to the surface, and finding a whole and healthy life.

The climb involves change; change always involves uncertainty, and with uncertainty comes fear and anxiety. Those of us who are long-term prisoners may feel safe with a life 'institutionalised' by depression: our routine and feelings are familiar. That life may not be comfortable, but it is recognisable; it is known, and so it feels safe.

Whatever baggage we carry – and we may be carrying more than one 'bag' – we need to be able to throw off whatever handicaps us, in order to make any progress in the climb out of depression. For some of us, there will be hard work to be done in addressing and managing the painful emotions that led us into the deep, dark hole in the first place. Those emotions aren't 'wrong', but out of place – they just lost their way.

Managing painful emotions

Thoughts and emotions can never be separated. They interact as electrochemical responses in the depths of our brain.

There are two important groups of emotions which directly affect our bodily functions, and also have a spiritual impact:
- *Fear-based emotions* are: anxiety, worry, resentment, frustration, impatience, annoyance, hate, anger, rage, resentment and guilt. These emotions result in a state of mind that produces an uncomfortable reaction in the body.
- *Faith-based emotions* are: 'love, joy, peace, patience, kindness, goodness, faithfulness, gentleness and self-control' (Gal. 5:22). These emotions produce a healthy state of mind and a *feel-good* factor in the body.

Emotions – whether they 'feel' good or bad – are part of the whole person God designed each of us to be. They have no value judgments attached: they just *are*. Labelling emotions as 'right' or 'wrong' inevitably leads to guilt – usually false guilt.

The key is to accept our emotions as part of our unique self, and learn how to manage them so that they don't manage us. If emotions are ignored or suppressed they will be buried alive and will inevitably surface – often at the most inappropriate moment, and in the most devastating way.

If we have grown up believing that it is wrong to express our emotions, then we may never have learnt how to do so appropriately, and would rather bury our feelings. But buried emotions can lead to depression. Accepting that I feel guilty, ashamed, sad or angry may be the first step to climbing out of depression.

Guilt

Guilt is one of the most complex and painful emotions to be found hidden within a depressed person.

The dictionary defines guilt as 'the fact or state of having offended'.[4] To be guilty is to be judged – by others or oneself – as having committed a crime or offence. Therefore, if our depression is caused by buried guilt, we will judge ourselves to have done something wrong in becoming depressed.

Guilt may be a remorseful awareness of having done something wrong, or self-reproach for supposed inadequacy or wrongdoing. We might also feel guilty because we don't live up to our own expectations, or our own high standards.

Guilt is designed by God to be a restraining and redeeming influence on fallen humanity. It *can* serve as a very helpful motivator in changing our behaviour. Equally, it can become a crippling prison of condemnation and torment; a handicap rather than a help.

We commonly say that guilt 'gnaws' at us, a word capturing the sense of something internal and inaccessible, which attacks relentlessly. Alternatively, guilt is seen as a burden that can never be shaken off. Other metaphors may describe guilt as 'a pebble in one's shoe', 'a throbbing phantom limb' or 'a torn ligament'.

Guilt can easily trigger shame and negativity when we are depressed. It is often heard as a message of disapproval from the conscience, which says, in effect: 'You should be ashamed of yourself.'

Shame

The word 'shame' comes from the Indo-European word 'skam', meaning to hide. It is defined as 'a feeling of distress or humiliation caused by consciousness of the guilt or folly of oneself or an associate'.

Guilt says 'I have *done* something wrong', whereas shame says '*I* am wrong'. While guilt relates to breaking laws or standards, shame is related to our very sense of self: 'I am ashamed of who I am.'

Shame is toxic, and often accompanied by painful feelings of alienation, self-doubt, loneliness, isolation and paranoia. It may show evidence of compulsive disorders, perfectionism, inferiority, inadequacy, failure, helplessness, hopelessness or narcissism, all of which can lead to depression.

In the Old Testament Job felt shame, whether he was guilty or not (Job 10:15). The psalmists often asked that they would not be put to shame (Psa. 25:2; 25:20; 31:17; 71:1). The New Testament brings us Jesus, who triumphed over shame even as He endured it. He scorned the shame of the cross: the shame that is, or should be, ours because of our wrongdoing. It was in the darkness of crucifixion that God did His greatest work through Jesus. Because of His death and resurrection, we do not have to stay in that dark place of shame (Heb. 13:12–14): He has redeemed it through God's grace and forgiveness, and brought us from darkness into light.

True guilt needs to be dealt with through that work done by Jesus. False guilt needs to be shown up for what it is by the light of God's forgiveness and grace.

Lorraine's younger sister Ruby died in a domestic accident when Lorraine was eight. Lorraine was chasing her sister in fun when a stair gate, designed to prevent falls, gave way. Lorraine blamed herself for the accident, into adulthood. Her parents rarely spoke about it through the years, too grief-stricken even to understand the reassurance needed by their surviving daughter. Lorraine's mother died when Lorraine was in her forties. Grief turned the underlying depression Lorraine had lived with for years into something deeper and darker, compounded by her earlier loss. As she struggled to cope, Lorraine's father, himself grieving, opened his heart to her, telling her that he had always blamed himself for Ruby's death: he felt that he should have regularly checked the stability of the stair gate. Recognising that father and daughter both needed help, their church minister arranged for specialist counselling at a Christian bereavement service where counsellors were accustomed to complicated grief. Father and daughter were supported as they slowly helped each other out of their guilt and depression. Lorraine later trained as a counsellor, and now works for the bereavement service that helped her and her father.

When we are depressed we often say that we feel 'flat', meaning our emotions are flattened. We may experience very little sense of fun, and feel as if we have lost the capacity to laugh. Life feels heavy: a drag. It may be that our mind is trying to avoid dealing with a deep sense of *sadness*: the loss of a loved one; the trauma of disease. Or perhaps it is trying to avoid dealing with internalised *anger*.

Sadness

Loss may cause depression when we shut out all sadness and grief in order to cope: 'I just have to get on with it.' This can happen in the short term – for example, as we 'get on with' organising a funeral, or feel we must 'stay strong' for other family members or friends. Often it is only once the funeral is over and everyone has gone back to their normal lives that the pain can be faced, and the real grieving process – allowing the sadness to come to the surface – can begin. Sometimes, that internalised sadness may continue for some time – often a near-lifetime – meaning that the grief remains unresolved until it is faced.

It is natural for others to want to try to make us feel happier when we are grieving, sad or depressed. But it may be more beneficial for us to be helped to get in touch with our sadness, and to be supported as we do so. Once the depth of our sadness has been experienced fully, we will not try to shut it out of our conscious thinking, but 'process' it in a healthy way that moves us forward so that we do not become 'stuck' in a place of grief and depression. (This is discussed in more detail in *An Insight into Bereavement*.[5])

Anger

We might be depressed because we are experiencing 'frozen rage',[6] that is, internalised anger. Anger is often the hidden flipside of the coin whose other side reads 'depression'.

Anger is a basic emotion, and feeling angry is as natural and necessary as feeling tired or hungry. It is part of an internal signalling system that alerts us to danger or need. Like every other emotion, anger is not 'wrong' – it just 'is'. Rather, it's how we deal with and express our anger that matters. Do we ignore it? Deny it? Stuff it down inside, and avoid it? Or do we face up to it and deal with it?

Some of us, especially those Christians who have been brought up to be 'meek and mild', believe that it is wrong to become openly angry – or even to feel angry. We will do almost anything to avoid confronting anger in ourselves or other people.

But the Bible tells us that God, while He is 'slow to anger' (Exod. 34:6; Psa. 86:15; 103:8) does often become angry – and expresses that anger (Exod. 32:10–19; 2 Kings 22:13), as did Jesus (John 2:13–16).

Anger often motivates us to take action and do what 'God require[s] of you' (Micah 6:8). The Jubilee 2000 campaign against world debt is an example, as are organisations like Hope for Justice. Anger at injustice and poverty causes us to take action.

It is important to acknowledge our feelings of personal anger, and learn to express that anger appropriately (Prov. 29:11; Eph. 4:26).

Practically, we might choose to:

- Rage at God (He knows everything about us anyway, and values our honesty!);
- Express our feelings by drawing or writing – destroying the result once the anger is vented;
- With the help of a counsellor, use soft toys to characterise our anger, or those we need to express our anger towards;
- Dance madly to very loud music!
- Play an aggressive sport like squash (taking care not to injure our opponent!);
- Chop wood, vacuum furiously, or pummel dough to make bread;
- Throw stones – well away from others! – perhaps into a lake or sea, letting the angry thoughts drop with the stones into the depths and be gone;
- Scream, for example in the middle of a field, where the sound does not disturb. Chris used to scream while cycling to work, letting the traffic noise drown her voice. She found that it was a safe way to express and let go of the anger she felt: anger arising from a sense of helplessness and powerless in having a daughter who was ill.

Most importantly, having vented our anger appropriately, we will need to move on to *forgive* where appropriate. Anger that does not lead to forgiveness – of self as well as others – will remain just that: anger. Like a weed left neglected, it will more than likely grow in stature and strength.

Anger is discussed more in Chris' book *An Insight into Anger* (Farnham: CWR, 2007).

Despair

Despair can envelop us like a deep and deadly darkness: a heaviness from which there seems to be no escape. It can be insidious and devious in its companionship, whispering: 'There's no way out, you know', or 'Surely it would be better to die?' Despair is an expert at mental torture, painting pictures of hopelessness and worst-case scenarios from which we feel unable to rid ourselves. Hazel Rolston, who suffered crippling postnatal depression and anxiety, writes that 'Despair's arguments seemed so plausible in the dark, murky atmosphere of the harsh environment.'[7]

If we are Christians, it is important to remind ourselves that any voice which tempts and taunts us is not from God and that its enticing commands, however well disguised, are not safe to follow. It is important to hold on to God, even though He seems lost or distant in the darkness. We can stay close to Him by keeping key Bible verses of assurance, security and love close at hand; and by asking a friend to 'look out for us' in this area, and pray for and with us. Hazel Rolston writes: 'I longed for someone to listen and spend time with me so that they would learn the language of my wild place and be able to understand my nuances of desperation.'[8] We can turn on the light in the middle of the night when all is threat and darkness; we can busy ourselves with something creative, or play a beautiful (but not mournful) piece of music.

Wendy has often found it helpful to remind herself that God is always closer than we think, and to dwell on Meister Eckhart's idea that God sometimes gives His presence away by 'clearing His throat' in the darkness we find ourselves in. For some time Wendy wondered why God needed to clear His throat. Then she realised that He was crying alongside her, and needed to clear His throat to shift the tears in order to speak. God does speak into the darkness, but not always in a way that we find easy to hear or understand.

We need to help one another come to terms with the fact that we all fall short as human beings, and that our vulnerabilities and weaknesses are common; we need to recognise that feelings and emotions are not an accurate guide to the sum of who we are as a whole. It's important to remind ourselves that each of us is not only accepted by God, but *loved* by Him beyond our understanding.

When our emotions are confused, our faith is often muddled too. If we have always depended on our emotions as a barometer of our lives, and rooted our identity in how 'I feel', then the enemy will find it easy to tease and torment us. Our emotions are subject to the subtle messages of events and memories, so our current emotional state is not an accurate measure of who we are.

Chris shares a simple modern parable which illustrates this point: there were three tightrope walkers – Faith, Emotion and Logic. 'When Emotion went first along the wire with Faith and Logic following, Emotion got very worried, wavered and fell off, dragging the other two down with him. When Logic went first with Faith second and Emotion bringing up the rear, everything was on a much more even keel. Emotion was steadied by the stabilising effect of the other two.'[9]

We can learn to unlock the buried feelings and emotions that we need to face up to by:

- Giving ourselves permission to feel the feeling at this moment. It is just that – a feeling.
- Noticing when our emotions are stirred, and asking ourselves:
  'What is going on within me that I am feeling so tense/angry/hurt?'

'How might my behaviour be protecting me from the uncomfortable emotions I need to address?'
- Using creativity to help ourselves get in touch with the buried feelings and emotions: art, drawing and writing.
- Seeking expert counselling and effective prayer for the healing of painful memories.

Once we are able to recognise our feelings, address them for what they are and work with them 'face to face', we will make progress in our climb out of depression.

Activity

Ask yourself:
  'How do I tend to deal with my emotions?'
  'Which of the emotions we have discussed have led me, or are most likely to lead me, into a place of depression?'
- Guilt
- Shame
- Anger
- Sadness
- Despair

Take five envelopes and a pad of sticky notes.

On each envelope write one of the 'emotion' words above – one envelope for each word. Keep the envelopes in a safe place and the notes close at hand. Over the next week, every time you feel depressed, briefly write how you feel, and why, on a sticky note. Try to identify which emotion is at the source of your low mood. Post your note into the appropriate envelope. As you do so, ask God to keep it for you until you can face it and deal with it. At the end of the week, arrange to spend some time with a member of your family, trusted friend or counsellor. Open your envelopes and 'unstick' your notes as you work – and pray – through each one. You should be able to identify clearly which emotions are most troublesome in triggering or worsening your depressed moods.

Consider practical ways to handle the most difficult emotions you face in a healthier way in future. Repeat the exercise – together or alone – for as long as you find it helpful.

Reflection

Often we compare ourselves to others where our emotions are concerned, thinking that we are more volatile, less patient or more moody than this or that person. Read the following words to remind yourself of your uniqueness:

> I am not off-the-peg – I am made-to-measure.
> No flat-pack 'me' has appeared on the shelf of
> humanity – I am bespoke.
> Bespoke by the creator God, no less!
> I am designed by one who does not make carbon
> copies or reproduced replicas.
> I was knit together in secret – yet nothing about me
> is a surprise.
> I am exactly as He planned: just who and what I
> should be – and am becoming even more the 'me'
> He intended.
> I am the sum of many parts – yet much more than
> their total.

No one else is exactly like me: my eyes, my
fingerprints, my DNA remind me.
I am unique.
Any complaints? Take them up with the maker!

Prayer

Creator God,
Thank You that You want to liberate my emotions
with Your love.
Set me free from my own failings and weaknesses.
Help me to see myself as You see me;
to value myself as Your child.
I bring these powerful – but precious – emotions to You
now, Lord God.
May I know true freedom.
Amen.

CHAPTER 4

Beginning to climb – Taking practical action

The practical steps that follow are only suggestions for a way forward. There are no guarantees built into them. They come with a realisation of just how difficult it can be, when depressed, to remember what day it is, let alone to follow a series of steps. Added to this, each one of us is unique, even in our experience of depression. Consequently, not everything that is included here will be feasible, possible or helpful for all of us, or for those we support.

However, if a desire to climb out of the pit of depression is heartfelt, we need to begin somewhere. We have already said that the first thing we need to do in order to begin the climb is to acknowledge the need for change, and to be prepared just to make a start. The key to change is within our grasp if we are willing to take the first step in changing how we see ourselves, others and the wider world, and to find God's place in our lives.

The final part of the chapter offers suggestions specifically for those who are accompanying others in their climb out of depression.

Step One: Managing physical symptoms

Sleep

First of all we need to pay attention to our sleep, because sleep is healing. Remember, when Elijah was depressed God first sent him to a place where he could sleep (1 Kings 19:5).

So, we might aim to:

- Set regular sleep times... and getting-up times.
- Have a 'winding-down' time before going to bed (read for a while, take a warm bath, or listen to relaxing music).
- Reduce caffeine and alcohol intake.
- Not remain sleepless in bed for more than 15 to 30 minutes, but get up and do something (preferably something boring like the ironing!) just for a short time, and then try to sleep again.
- Pay attention to dreams. Nightmares and recurring dreams may be symbolic of our inner struggles, or may point to the unfinished business of our emotions. It might help to jot a few details down on waking, and/or share them with someone who will pray through the dream with us, or who has had training in dream therapy.

Healthy eating

When we are depressed, our eating can become chaotic. We may eat erratically, at odd times of day and night; nibble whatever is 'easiest' or to hand; not eat at all, or eat too much – often 'comfort eating'.

If we pay attention to our diet and maintain regular mealtimes, we will give our day 'shape'. If we spend time doing something creative or useful – including trying new recipes or foods – we may begin to look forward to mealtimes again. If we can include 'five a day' portions of fruit and vegetables and drink plenty of water, we will begin to feel better physically, too.

Appearance and dress

When we are depressed, we often neglect our appearance. Wearing dark, drab colours reflects our inner world, and we don't bother to make ourselves look attractive or even presentable – a woman may give up on her hair; a man may not bother shaving – because we don't feel there is anything attractive about us. It's important that we break the cycle of gloom, make ourselves look good, and choose something colourful to wear.

Chris heard the story of a very depressed woman who only wore black – usually tracksuit bottoms and a drab top. Her clinical psychologist spotted a creative side to his client's personality, and suggested that she might try experimenting with the clothes she wore. He encouraged her to be as outrageous or creative as she liked – to surprise him, perhaps. At first she simply wore a brighter top, then she became braver, wearing something more adventurous or humorous at each appointment – to the delight of both client and helper! As a result the woman not only began to know – and share – joy, but she began taking an interest in her clothes again, leaving the tracksuit bottoms behind. It was a small but important step on her way to recovery.

Exercise

Exercise has proven benefits for all of us – whether we are depressed or not. It is often described as an anti-depressant, because physical exertion prompts the release of endorphins in our brain which give us the 'feel-good' factor. The key is to choose a form of exercise we enjoy – not one that we feel we 'ought' to do! The best activities are those we can share with others – preferably outside in the fresh air. There's no need to rush off to join an expensive gym: a walk in the park, or along a beach with a friend, can be just as beneficial, if not more so.

Exercise:

• releases feelings of tension, frustration and anger
• increases the amount and quality of sleep
• raises energy levels
• builds self-esteem and confidence by helping improve muscle tone
• releases endorphins – often known as a the 'happy hormones' – which makes us feel better.

Step Two: Managing our behavioural patterns

When depression leaves us feeling overwhelmed by life, withdrawal is a common response – but it is counterproductive. Withdrawal keeps us locked in the isolation that exacerbates our depression, maintaining a vicious circle of loneliness and self-absorption. It's all too easy to sleep late, watch daytime TV, and leave the phone or doorbell unanswered. People seem to be too much effort, so we avoid them. Then we realise they have stopped calling, and we think they 'don't care'! The more we become locked into ourselves, the more we slow down, feel tired, and lose the inclination to be active. As our activity level drops, our confidence is further reduced, and we drift downward in what is called 'the lethargy spiral'. The more we don't do anything, the more we have difficulty in finding energy to do anything.

We need to recognise the lethargy spiral (shown in the

diagram opposite) that we can so easily be caught in, and understand how our negative thoughts maintain that cycle, sustaining or increasing our depression:

The Cycle of Lethargy

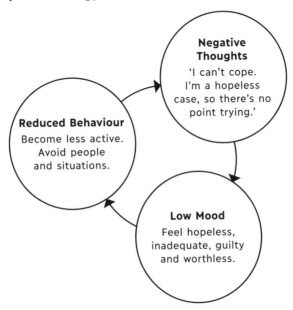

If we are to re-engage with life 'on the surface', we need to re-engage with people and with purpose. Therefore, the next step might be to break the lethargy cycle and build some form of activity into our daily life.

Activity gives us a useful purpose, a clear focus, and a reason for 'being'. It distracts us from the downward spiral of negative thinking, and stimulates us mentally. Completing a task or finishing an activity gives us a sense of achievement, building our self-esteem and confidence. Engaging in activities with others adds extra dimensions: companionship, conversation, laughter, and often a sense of teamwork and service to others. It can be quite an effort to get involved in 'doing things' again when we've been depressed. But if we choose the right activity, with someone who understands where we are and what we need, it can make a tremendous difference to our mood.

The *worst thing* we can do is to sit alone for hours to ruminate. The *best thing* we can do is say, 'Yes, I'll try that.'

Step Three: Reactivating our life: Goal-setting

Once we have recognised the need for exercise, sleep, company, a healthy diet and some purpose – and taken all these steps – we are beginning to make progress.

At this point, it may help to begin an activity with clearly defined goals, to assist our climb out of lethargy and depression.

A word of caution: a long list of aims, activities, goals and tasks may be daunting if we are not ready to move on, or if we try to tackle too much alone. So it might be helpful to ask a friend to sit down with us and help us to make sense of the next stage of our climb: they can help us to choose or prioritise some of the tasks included below. The idea of goal-setting is to aim for and reach a small, achievable goal – not to trip up as soon as the starting-gun is fired!

Goal-setting (perhaps with a friend or counsellor)

First, we...

- Make a list of the *tasks* we have stopped doing since becoming depressed, for example making phone calls, doing our hair, shaving, washing clothes, doing housework;
- Put these tasks in order of priority. Which one needs to be done first? Which one do I realistically think I can do today? You could number them 1, 2, 3. (There are no 'rights' or 'wrongs' in this activity, just your choices.)

As we do this, it might be helpful to ask: 'Am I a morning person or an evening person? When is my energy level at its highest? Can I arrange to complete these tasks at a time when I'm on top of things?'

Secondly, we set *goals* for the week – a balance of goals that are both achievable and pleasurable.

We might choose the first *goal*, such as 'Start doing housework again', break it down into achievable *objectives*, for example 'Keep the lounge tidy', and build up gradually. So, start with a simple task, like vacuuming the carpet, and decide in advance how often to do it, and when. Set simple goals to begin with, in order to keep anxiety levels down, and also to make goals and objectives achievable and affirming. The last thing we want is to be more depressed because there is so much to do, and we haven't done any of it!

Our goal list might look something like this:

Stopped or reduced activities	Goal
· Stayed in bed all morning	· Get up one hour earlier each day this week
· Stopped phoning friends	· Phone one friend every Wednesday
· Haven't dealt with finances	· Every Friday morning spend twenty minutes sorting out which bills need paying
· Stopped doing exercise	· Take a five-minute walk three times a week: Monday, Wednesday, Saturday

Next, we carry out the tasks to achieve our objectives and meet our goals.

If we have difficulty completing a task (eg vacuuming), achieving an objective (keeping the lounge tidy) or reaching a goal (resuming housework chores), we may need to consider whether that goal is set too high, given our current energy levels and mood.

Remember: our aim is for *simple, achievable goals*. The most important thing is to make a start. As our mood improves, so will our energy level and our sense of achievement. Only as we recognise improvement should we step up our activity, adding more tasks, objectives and goals.

It's important to remember that climbing out of depression may mean taking three steps up and two steps back down. The important thing is that we are still moving, still climbing.

The final step is to congratulate ourselves when a goal is reached: just ticking off the tasks from a short list can give us a real sense of achievement.

At the end of a week, we can appraise last week's goals and set new ones for the next week. We might ask: 'Do I want to maintain these goals? If so, why? Do I want to lower my goals, because I couldn't reach them last week? Am I ready to make my goals a little more challenging? Is there enough time for rest and relaxation, or am I putting too much pressure on myself too soon?'

Keeping track of progress

When we're depressed, it's hard to believe that we're achieving anything, so it may be helpful to keep a simple list of the things we *do* achieve. We could even give them a star rating, eg 'ironing***', or jot down how we felt while we were working or once we'd achieved something, for example 'It gave me a real buzz to see a neat pile of ironed shirts!'

The key to making progress is to maintain a balance between challenge and achievement: setting ourselves tasks that stretch us a little, without causing stress or a sense of failure. That's why it's so helpful to have a friend with us when we tackle some activities. A friend can encourage us, prod us a bit, be there if things do go a bit 'pear-shaped' – and remind us to do something pleasurable! It helps us to gain a reward for our effort.

Managing a balanced life

As we begin the climb out of depression, we need to avoid putting too much pressure on ourselves to 'get better'. A slow, steady climb with a few slips back a rung or two is far better than a desperate scrabble upwards followed by a hard fall.

Perhaps the most important thing we can do is to enlist support from someone who will stick with us all the way: someone who will offer us a balance of understanding, challenge and encouragement. Some of us may find that support within our family, for others that person may be a friend at work, at church or in a club, society or support group.

As we make progress, it's helpful to make time to review progress: to ask if we are taking opportunities to spend time with friends and family; to enjoy quiet time alone, and fun time with others; to eat well, take regular exercise, and enjoy hobbies and wider interests.

For some of us, that might include paid work, volunteering or service: activities which give us a sense of worth and achievement, and enable us to use our gifts. We are aiming for a balanced life which reminds us every day that we are unique, that we are precious and honoured in God's sight – and that He loves us: 'you are precious and honoured in my sight, and... I love you' (Isa. 43:4).

Climbing companions: helping someone else who is depressed

When we want to help someone else who is depressed we need to follow the rule of every good first aider, and protect ourselves first. If I want to assist someone who is involved in a road traffic accident I will not wander out into the middle of the road without making sure that an oncoming car won't hit me! Depression can sometimes be infectious – or seductive. We must do all we can to prevent the other person, or their depression, from pulling us down with them, whether intentionally or not. We need to adopt an approach of 'empathy + structure', establishing clear boundaries for our involvement and support.

It's easy to promise to 'always come when you want me', without considering what that means for our own lives and family. It's much better to commit ourselves to manageable support than to promise the earth and then give up, leaving the depressed person unsupported because we can no longer cope. A co-operative 'team' approach, with trusted friends sharing support for a depressed person, often works well.

Ruth suffered depression after the breakdown of her marriage, and leant heavily on her friends. She would go from one to another demanding considerable attention and support, while each friend thought that she was the only one helping. When three of these friends got together they realised what was happening, and, after consultation with a few others, decided on a plan of action that would offer Ruth all the care and support she needed, but would not exhaust them all. They told Ruth that one friend would be available for taking her to church, one for company on long evenings, one for helping with the housework and shopping, and so on. They wondered if Ruth would feel they were being harsh, but she simply felt they were caring for her in a really organised way! Once Ruth felt able to cope again, the friendships were able to return to a more natural footing. But the friends had learnt much from the experience – as much about their own needs as about Ruth's.

Once we have set clear boundaries, we can focus on the needs of the person.

Being there

We can support a depressed person by:

- Lessening their isolation with frequent brief visits, walking with them, making hot drinks or snacks, cooking them a meal, being in a room nearby, sitting with them doing something quietly, or talking/listening when they want.
- Reminding them how much they are valued, particularly through our smiles and voice and, if appropriate, telling them occasionally how much we love them.
- Not telling them to 'pull themselves together' or reproaching them for being ill or difficult – however tempted we might be!
- Not trying to 'cheer them up' as we would someone who is temporarily sad or discouraged. This can be very isolating for the person we are supporting, as it compounds the belief that 'nobody understands'.
- Taking care in our use of the language of sickness and health. The depressed person is going through an experience that most people encounter at some point in their lives. They *can* emerge stronger and wiser.
- Remembering that a depressed person is trying to survive as a person. As a result, their focus may – temporarily – be totally self-centred.

It's often hard to 'be there' for a depressed person. They will often struggle to talk, leaving a heavy and awkward silence. We may worry about what they are thinking, may not know where to focus our gaze, or try to dismiss our fears by filling the space with trivial chat – but that's not always helpful. Just being there can be enough.

Often a depressed person will find the busyness of others

difficult: it reminds them of their own paralysis of activity, their lack of motivation, or the absence of 'normal life'. Noise and activity may be distressing for them. Others may be reassured by having someone nearby. It may be wise just to *ask*: 'Is it OK if I do this?' or 'Would it help if I sit here for a while?'

Sometimes it is helpful to go for a walk or a drive together: there are incidental details to comment upon, both of you are 'doing' something, conversation can be as deep or mundane as needed – and the fresh air or change of scene is a bonus. Wendy remembers her dad lovingly driving her around the prettiest of Kent and Sussex churches when she was depressed as a teenager. Not much was said of any consequence, but she still recalls, thirty years on, just how much that outing – marked by acceptance, love and shared moments of gentle joy – helped her. In later years, when Wendy was suffering from postnatal depression, a friend who called round and did some ironing helped in a similar way. Wendy needed to hear all the news, and to know that life was going on normally for everyone else. As her friend ironed, a chore was completed, the chat was comfortingly familiar, and it was gratifying for her friend to know she was doing something to help.

Maintaining awareness

However we listen or seek to help the depressed person, let's remain *aware*.

Firstly, it's important to be aware of their level of despair, and quick to urge professional help if we think they may be suicidal – and certainly if they mention thinking about ending their life. Even a passing remark can be an indication that suicide has been considered. The rage we may pick up from someone who is depressed may be directed at themselves, or someone else. Is the depressed person a danger to either? If they seem to get worse, it's important to encourage them to visit their doctor – perhaps accompanying them – and encourage them to follow the prescribed treatment.

Secondly, let's be aware of the need to respect personal space: we may offer a hug, only to get a chilly response. A depressed person is not always receptive to physical contact, even to a hand held out, or a pat on the shoulder. Feelings of love or affection may not be available to them. It's hard not to feel that any anger the person expresses is directed at us personally, yet often it is those who are closest who bear the brunt of the pain and frustration.

Thirdly, therefore, we need to be aware of the impact of depression on close family and friends. If the depressed person is a family member we may feel we are trying to avoid 'walking on eggshells', or to prevent a spirit of gloom affecting the whole family. But it's important that we don't allow the individual's state to monopolise the space in the home, or dominate the atmosphere. Children need to be allowed to carry on as usual, laughing and playing, not tip-toeing fearfully around the depressed person. Other family members must give themselves permission to carry on with their own lives.

Celebrity chef Rick Stein has shared the story of his own childhood,[1] and the impact his father's bipolar disorder had on the family. He mentions that as children 'we never knew how he would be' – sociable, or deep in despair. Rick paints a picture of his mother quietly battling to hold a family together and keep a husband alive, while maintaining a normal life for everyone.

It's important that we are self-aware, acknowledging a sense of helplessness in ourselves if that is our experience. There is a limit to what we can do to help. We cannot rescue a friend or family member who is depressed. They have to want to find a way out for themselves. We may think we can see that way clearly – but perhaps they cannot. This may be very frustrating for us: and our frustration needs to be acknowledged and accepted. Moreover, as carers we may feel drained of loving-kindness and filled with a strong sense of frustration, irritation, anger and impatience. Such feelings are entirely normal, and we may need to find our own support in dealing with them.

Finally, we need to be aware of the changes which may occur as a result of depression, including consequent problems with relationships. Depression changes the sufferer – both during and after the experience, and often for the better. But in rigid families there may be fearfulness if one member changes – even if that change is positive. When a person emerges from depression there may be tension and conflict, a sense of jostling as positions are changed or roles are resumed – particularly if other family members don't want to adapt. For example, a daughter may want her younger sister to continue to be depressed so that she won't have any competition; a wife may have enjoyed being head of the family while her husband has been depressed. Family members may use the depressed person as a scapegoat or an excuse for their own questionable behaviour, or blame them for unrelated events and circumstances. Relatives may even continue to undermine a depressed person's self-confidence, and prevent them from emerging transformed. The depressed person needs to be given freedom to change into the person they can truly become. Perhaps this sense of the individual's potential is where our awareness needs to be most acute.

What we can offer as carer and friend

Value and acceptance

We can show value and acceptance by offering unconditional love. People often hate themselves when they are depressed. They feel guilty, they blame themselves, and they have low self-esteem: their sense of worth will only be regained when they feel valued and accepted. We demonstrate acceptance when we avoid being judgmental; when we listen as an equal; when we avoid reminding them of other's people's suffering (this will only increase their self-hatred); and when we accept their place of self-centredness – without saying so!

Empathy and hope

We offer empathy when we find the most appropriate way to say 'I sense that this is a really difficult place for you to be, and that it seems there is no way out'. We offer hope when we say 'Everything passes, nothing lasts forever'. We should try not to offer 'advice' even if we can see a way through, but help the depressed person to find that way through for themselves – even if they need to do so clutching our hand, figuratively or otherwise. When they start to feel better we can put positive things into the empty space left by depression, gently encouraging them to share happy memories – photo albums are helpful here – giving them something to look forward to, and helping them know that life can be good again.

Practical help

The best practical help is more than just 'doing'. It is motivated by loving, caring, and a desire to see restoration. Preparing meals, shopping, minding the children, housework, administrative tasks or letter-writing, going for a walk or swim together may all help. Think twice about telling a depressed person what to do, or trying to 'take over', but tentatively offer help. It's important that we let them choose to accept or reject our offer, thus giving them a sense of control over their lives. It's also not helpful to load them with guilt when they *haven't* managed to do something (they know that!), or put pressure on them when they *have* done it: 'I told you, you'd enjoy the fresh air' – spoken with the irritating condescension of Joyce Grenfell or Hyacinth Bucket!

Depressed people often feel very guilty at the amount of help they need, and we can add to their guilt by making our help seem burdensome. But if we are helping/calling in/doing an errand for them, on our way somewhere else, we can send the message that we are taking their situation in our stride *and* accepting both their value as a person and their need for help.

By contrast, it is easy to get caught in the 'yes… but' game if the depressed person tells us why our idea will *not* help: 'I've done that before and it didn't work' needs a change of direction in the conversation. A guilty 'You needn't do that, I can manage' (when they obviously can't) might be avoided by a change of approach, implying generosity rather than extra effort on our part: 'I'll make your meal tonight shall I? I always cook too much anyway!'

Conversation

Most people like sharing their thoughts, feelings and fears with a good listener, because it affirms their existence and their worth. So, however hard – and however often – we've heard the 'story', we may have to hear it again. In fact, we may be called on to listen ten times as much as we talk.

It can be helpful for the depressed person to talk about an issue which looks very different 'in the light' to how they see it 'in the dark'. But it is important that the issue discussed is not presented as having a 'right' or 'wrong' answer. Our judgment-free conversation may help the depressed person to see their options more clearly.

Where conversation – or lack of it – is concerned, we should encourage ourselves. Often we will sit and listen to someone who is depressed, not knowing what to say, and leave feeling as if we have been no use at all. Then suddenly, we will hear the words 'Thank you – you've helped me so much!' and think, 'But I didn't say a word!' Sometimes, just being there – and listening – is enough.

Sitting with someone quietly also gives them the message that they are of value. Chris once heard a pastor say that when he was deeply depressed, one of his most treasured memories of kindness was of a friend who came regularly just to sit with him in silence, making no demands upon him. The pastor pointed out that when people are dying, the first thing they want to do is to sit with their loved ones and hold their hand. In a similar way, when a person is depressed, your just being there and sitting with them whilst they take the long road to recovery is tremendously appreciated. Chris's daughter remembers that when she was ill with depression her dad sat with her, expecting no exchange of words but just holding her hand. It was a great comfort to her.

Companionship in the choppy waters of faith

A depressed person may begin to test their faith: 'Why has God left me? Where is He?' We need to remember, and to communicate, that doubt is not the opposite of faith – it is *part* of faith. The greatest biblical lives show evidence of doubt. Jesus never squashed or berated a genuine doubter – He always commended people for whatever faith they had, while encouraging them to have more faith.

Be careful not to make assumptions about a depressed person's standing before God, for example suggesting 'Your faith is faltering, so we don't think you're a Christian any more', or demanding 'Repent… you are in sin!' (Sadly, such responses do happen!) There is nothing more demoralising to a depressed Christian than the hostility and criticism of other Christians who have never experienced depression, and who don't have the love or compassion to stay alongside in an attempt to understand. Christian doctrine has a place, but acceptance, understanding and love are more important to a depressed person.

Depression is *never* God's way of punishing us for something we have done wrong. We may separate ourselves from Him through our own wilfulness or weakness – but God does not *punish* with depression or illness. Job's 'comforters' fell into the trap of believing that Job was to blame for his terrible afflictions. He wasn't: God was allowing the enemy to test him – and God knew what the outcome would be.

Suggesting 'inspirational' verses or 'challenging' books for the depressed person to read may or may not be helpful. Carefully chosen Bible-reading notes, simple cards carrying single verses, or booklets designed for new Christians, might help. The latter can remind us of the basis of our faith when we feel the foundations tremble. But we shouldn't assume that the individual's faith is wavering. Those who are depressed may still find great comfort in God, identification with their situation in the Psalms, and an understanding of being 'lifted... out of the slimy pit' (Psa. 40:2; 103:4). We should listen, learn – and be slow to judge. God still has His hand on the life of the person before us, and He is perfecting His plan for them.

(Chapter 6 looks in more detail at the relationship between faith, depression and spiritual darkness.)

Activity

If you are depressed yourself: Ask a friend, partner or carer to help you to work through the goal-setting exercises in this chapter.

If you are supporting someone who is depressed: Which practical steps or suggestions might you put into practice... today?... This week?

Reflection

Reflect on Paul's words in 2 Corinthians 1:3–4:

> Praise be to the God and Father of our Lord Jesus Christ, the Father of compassion and the God of all comfort, who comforts us in all our troubles, so that we can comfort those in any trouble with the comfort we ourselves have received from God.

How do these verses guide us in the way we support one another – and seek support – in the suffering of depression?

How might these words offer hope to those who are 'beginning the climb' out of depresion?

Prayer

Lord,
There is a reason why You designed us to walk the way we do:
One foot in front of the other; step by step.
That is all You ask of me:
To take a step – my hand clasped in yours – as the gloom
slowly lifts.
Make me brave, Lord.
Help me take the first steps.
Walk with me.
Amen.

CHAPTER 5

Continuing the climb –
Managing our thinking

Our thinking generally provides a commentary for our lives, like a radio playing in the background. If our emotional state is healthy we can adjust the content and volume at will. But when we are depressed, our thinking dictates our response to just about everything that happens to us. Our interpretations of life experiences give them meaning. But we create that meaning through our guesses, assumptions and theories about what is going on around us, and by evaluating what is said and done by us and by others. Our skewed thinking very often maintains our depression and feeds it. The lethargy cycle, in the previous chapter, showed how our negative thoughts maintain this cycle. Every thought has an electrochemical reaction in our brain, so happy thoughts release chemicals called endorphins which give us the 'feel-good factor', whereas negative thoughts release different chemicals which lower our mood. Consequently, learning to manage our thinking rather than allowing our thinking to manage *us* is essential for a steady climb out of depression.

The first thing we need to understand is that our perception and understanding of events – and consequently what we think about those events – is often faulty. Consider the following scenario, reported from Janet's perspective:

> Janet is walking down the street and sees her friend
> Karen on the other side of the road. Janet shouts out,
> 'Hi' but Karen does not respond. Janet's first thought is:
> 'Oh dear, I must have done something wrong. Karen is
> ignoring me.' Janet's heart sinks, she begins to feel low,
> her self-esteem plummets, and she walks home searching
> her memory for the 'thing' she might have 'done' to
> offend Karen and put their friendship at risk.

Notice that Janet's focus was instantly drawn to *herself* – not to her friend. If Janet's perception had been different she might have thought: 'Poor Karen, she must have something important on her mind. Perhaps she's had a rotten time with her son again? I'll call her later.' Here, Janet's perception would be one of concern – the focus on her friend, not on herself.

How we see things makes a huge difference to our thinking: a simple event can be interpreted differently because of a change in perception. Some years ago the cover photograph on one side of a popular book showed a young man running at some speed towards an elderly lady who was about to cross the road. At first glance, the assumption was that the young man was about to snatch the handbag that the elderly woman was holding somewhat distractedly. But the other side of the book cover revealed the whole picture: it was clear that the young man was running in order to prevent the woman from walking into the path of an out-of-control van, whose approach she hadn't noticed. Sometimes we need to wait until we have a complete picture in order to fully understand what we are seeing.

Although people may see the same objects and experience the same events – often with a shared response – there will always be individual differences as we each process the world in unique ways. Our thoughts shape our world, so depressive thoughts – arising from biased and negative interpretation – will shape our world negatively. If we are depressed we will be quick to judge ourselves unfairly and harshly, focusing on the negative and ignoring the positive. We will view the situations we face in an unrealistically pessimistic way, dismissing the hopeful aspects, and we will envisage a difficult, disappointing or hopeless future. Our thinking may even damage our health. The American Psychologist Dr Caroline Leaf says that research has shown that 'around 87 per cent of illnesses can be attributed to our thought life and about 13 per cent to genetics and environment'.[1]

When depressed, we will move from the occasional wander into negativity that all of us experience, to a total pattern of distorted and negative thinking. Such thinking patterns are many and varied. The following features combine to create a smothering patchwork of negative thought:

- *Over-generalisation*: we make one mistake and assume that an entire project will fail, or we have difficulty with one person and assume that the whole world is against us: 'They all hate me.'
- *All-or-nothing thinking*: we oversimplify all that happens into black or white, with no shades of grey: 'I didn't get the job – I must be unemployable.'
- *Blowing things out of proportion*: every small problem becomes a mountain; every word – or silence – from others is loaded with imagined negative meaning: 'The boiler doesn't work... we'll need a new one... we can't afford it... we'll be ruined'; 'she hasn't phoned me for ages... she doesn't like me... that friendship is over... nobody likes me.'
- *Labelling*: we call ourselves names – *silly cow; stupid; failure* – believing that these labels describe us; we enlarge

the description: 'I'm so useless – how could I expect them to like my work?'

- *Self-blame*: whatever the situation and wherever responsibility lies, we blame ourselves: 'It's my fault, I shouldn't have come.'
- *Filtering*: we only see our mistakes and weaknesses, not our accomplishments and strengths; we ignore the good and see only the bad: 'I got six "Excellent" grades on my feedback form, and one "Quite good"! What did I do wrong?'
- *Disqualifying the positive*: anything positive is discounted with a negative thought: 'It's not as good as they said it was: I made a mistake with this... and this... and this could have been better.'
- *Mind-reading*: we believe we know what other people are thinking about us – and it must be negative. So we react to what we imagine they're thinking, without finding out the truth: 'She must think I'm too big for my boots because I'm leading this session.'
- *Fortune-telling*: we think we know what the future holds, and it's not good: 'This will never work out for me. I never get any good results in life.'
- *Rigid thinking*: we chastise ourselves because 'I should be like this', and 'the world ought to be like that'; the underlying assumption is that 'things will never improve.'

'Nats' (negative automatic thoughts) are not the result of conscious reasoning or decision-making, and may be so automatic that they are difficult to identify. They seem to jump into our mind from nowhere – even when things are going well. It's as if these 'nats' conspire, choosing to ambush us when we are most vulnerable.

Self-criticism

Self-criticism is often the 'nat' which holds all the other 'nats' together. It is a common symptom of depression that can 'lock us in' to ourselves.

If we constantly criticise and condemn ourselves, we begin to feel low. Likewise, if we accept the criticism we hear from others without question, it becomes self-belief because we never stop to consider whether it is fair. We hear the echoes of that same criticism whenever we fail, and are far too hard on ourselves as a result, falling into 'black and white' thinking. We interpret every innocent mistake as serious failure, and even positive comments and compliments are suspicious to us. We internalise our self-condemnation to the point that we listen to nothing else.

We may have to work hard to resist the taunting of our self-critical voice, identify our negative thought patterns, and note the recurring situations which cause us to self-condemn. Keeping a diary may help. If we can identify those situations and events that are likely to trigger a negative thought, we can consciously rehearse a new, more realistic and positive thought beforehand.

There are several ways of managing critical and negative thoughts. One or more of these approaches may be helpful in reversing the downward spiral of negativity so common in depression.

For more detail on how to tame our inner critical voice, read Chris' book *An Insight into Self-Acceptance* (Farnham: CWR, 2016).

Recognising strongholds

Negative thought patterns often have such a strong hold over us that we cannot break them on our own. The Bible refers to such situations as just that – 'strongholds': 'For though we live in the world, we do not wage war as the world does. The weapons we fight with are not the weapons of the world. On the contrary, they have divine power to demolish strongholds' (2 Cor. 10:3–4).

The writer of those words, Paul, uses the word 'stronghold' to define the 'spiritual fortresses' in which the enemy, Satan, hides. These fortresses exist in the thought patterns and attitudes that govern what we do and say. Therefore, an unhealthy stronghold is 'any type of thinking that exalts itself above the knowledge of God, thereby giving the enemy a secure place of influence in an individual's thought life'.[2] Paul goes on to suggest that we 'take captive every thought to make it obedient to Christ' (v5).

> Sue grew up with an alcoholic father who was drunk and aggressive almost every day. She hid under her bed when he came home, in order to avoid conflict. Sue's defensive reaction formed patterns of wrong thinking and behaviour, as she learned to do and say anything to keep the peace. Fifteen years on, these deeply ingrained patterns had formed strongholds in her mind. Sue was depressed, feeling just as trapped, in a marriage to an abusive and critical husband. Fear of conflict made her feel unable to leave, and she also felt 'worthless'.
>
> In counselling, Sue was encouraged to recognise and dismantle the strongholds of negative thought, taking

every thought 'captive'; holding it before Christ with the question 'Is this true?' As she worked through her thoughts, with repentance where necessary, she began to understand God's view of her, and gradually learnt to balance self-critical, judgmental thoughts with thoughts of self-acceptance and kindness. Once the strongholds were broken, Sue built up enough God-centred strength to enable her to move forward, and out of her abusive marriage.

It is repentance and release – letting go – of wrong attitudes and self-beliefs which begins the process of breaking down strongholds:

Firstly, we acknowledge and accept our hurt, anxiety and depression, and identify our thoughts for what they are. Our negative thought may be, 'I am worthless'.

Secondly, we take this thought 'captive', by asking: 'Does God say that about me?' We answer: 'No, He doesn't'.

Thirdly, we repent and express to God a heartfelt desire to change, and to let go of wrong thoughts about ourselves. Psalm 51 will help us: 'Have mercy on me, O God, according to your unfailing love; according to your great compassion blot out my transgressions.' We are specific in confessing our sin: 'I confess that I have labelled myself as "worthless", and repent of the wrong belief that I am worthless.' It can be hard to accept that this attitude is a 'wrong' thought that needs to be repented of. But it is contrary to what God clearly tells us about ourselves, it denies His unconditional love and therefore, in this sense, it is a wrong thought: a thought which needs the liberation of repentance and forgiveness.

Fourthly, we receive God's love and forgiveness, asking Him to strengthen us in our thoughts, behaviour and emotions, knowing that 'If we confess our sins, he is faithful and just and will forgive us our sins' (1 John 1:9).

Lastly, we choose to let go of the lie we have believed about ourselves, and choose to replace that lie with God's truth, asking God to renew our heart, mind, emotions and will through the empowerment of the Holy Spirit, remembering that 'you are precious and honoured in my sight and... I love you' (Isa. 43:4), and that 'God so loved the world that he gave his one and only Son' for us (John 3:16).

Our goal is to grow into wholeness, opening ourselves up to God and allowing His Spirit to bring healing. When we are depressed it is easy for our emotional brain to disregard what God says about us and our worth. Therefore, it is important to bring more balance to our thoughts – to let God 'tip the balance', if you like.

Once we have imprinted God's truth about us on our minds, we can ask ourselves the following questions in order to think more balanced, realistic thoughts:

- What is the result of my distorted thinking?
- What evidence do I have to support this negative thought?
- What evidence do I have that doesn't support this thought?
- What does this negative thought say about me and my life?
- What does God say about me and my life?
- What does this thought say about my future?
- What is God's truth about this situation, about me and my future?

In this way we can find new, alternative, balanced thoughts.

Sue (in the story on page 96) was encouraged to find a 'new' thought based on real evidence, not on distorted thinking. Sue's new, alternative thinking developed like this:

Thought	Evidence	Alternative, balanced thought
I am worthless.	My friends say they always enjoy time spent with me. My husband never says anything nice about me.	My close friends seem to enjoy my company and value my friendship, even though my husband doesn't. I am worth everything to God because Jesus died for me.
If I were different my husband wouldn't get angry.	He's always trying to control everyone – and it's not just me he shouts at.	I'm not going to take this personally. How he reacts to my sincere attempts to run a home is his responsibility, not mine. I am not going to draw my identity from what he says about me.
I am a failure. Whatever I do for my husband is not good enough for him.	I work hard and I do my best.	I am going to accept that God says that my best is good enough for Him. God says I am 'precious' to Him and I am 'the apple of His eye'.

In conclusion, one of Sue's original thoughts was 'I am worthless'. Her new thought became 'I am precious to God'. 'I am useless' became 'I work hard and do my best. If that best is good enough for God, it's good enough for me.'

(See Appendix 2 for the simple outline of a 'thought diary' like Sue's.)

Recognising the positive (looking for non-confirming evidence)

Once negative thoughts are challenged and 'put in their place', we want to replace them with something better.

We mentioned earlier that when we are depressed our brain filters out the positive, and only notices the negative. If something good happens or something positive is said, we discount it. To overcome this negative thinking pattern, it may help to keep a note of the good things that happen in our lives in order to develop a more realistic and balanced view of ourselves and our situation.

Writing down the positive words spoken, the incident or occasion when things went well – however trivial each may seem – enables us to maintain a permanent, positive record which we can refer back to on the not-so-good days.

It might be helpful to record occasions when:

- someone compliments us;
- we enjoy an unexpected friendly exchange;
- we have done something worthwhile for somebody else;
- something we have worked at has a good outcome;
- friends chat with us and leave us feeling good about ourselves;
- we experience something particularly kind or uplifting in the human world;
- we notice something beautiful or surprising in the natural world around us.

Too often we are so busy looking out for the negatives, that we sweep the positives aside.

Addressing our negative thinking: Kindness and compassion to self

Learning to have compassion for oneself is as important as having compassion for others. Paul Gilbert, a psychologist and author of *The Compassionate Mind,*[3] says 'compassion can help us heal our turbulent minds and enhance our well-being'. It is a skill that can be learned.

When depressed, we often judge ourselves more harshly than we would ever judge others. Yet Scripture teaches us to love our neighbours as we love ourselves. Do we *really* love ourselves with the same love that we give away to others? The Bible records numerous instances of Jesus' compassion. He remains understanding and kind towards us, with all our shortcomings and inadequacies. Self-compassion means treating ourselves in the same way, with God's love and acceptance. Finding a compassionate voice which silences our critical voice enables us to gradually give up self-criticism and self-condemnation, because 'Therefore, there is now no condemnation for those who are in Christ Jesus' (Rom. 8:1).

In order to find a compassionate voice, we can try working through the following process:

The negative thought ambushes us: 'I can't do this, I'm useless.'

Firstly, as we hear our negative voice, we ask ourselves; 'Would a caring mother or friend say that?' We might say: 'I know you're scared, but I'll be there encouraging you. Let's do it step by step;' noting the understanding, kindness and care the voice communicates.

Secondly, we ask ourselves: 'How can I comfort and care for myself as a caring mother or friend would care for me in this moment?' Or we might ask: 'What would other people say about the thought "I can't do this, I'm useless"? Would they say it was true? What kind of words would I like to hear?' Then we might speak those alternative words to ourselves: 'Come on, you can cope. Think how good you were when X happened and Y went wrong. You're more capable than you think! Just do this bit by bit. You'll get there.'

Thirdly, we remember that God does not condemn us, but accepts us lovingly with open arms, even though He knows everything about us. He says, 'I have drawn you with loving-kindness' (Jer. 31:3); 'My grace is sufficient for you' (2 Cor. 12:9); 'And the peace of God, which transcends all understanding, will guard your hearts and your minds' (Phil. 4:7). If we imagine, and 'hear' deep in our heart, what God the Father and Son might say to us in this particular situation, and we imagine someone speaking like that to us in a gentle voice, we can experience 'kindness to self'.

Accepting that we are all fallible human beings, mortal and imperfect, is an important part of having compassion for ourselves. It means accepting and loving ourselves just as God loves and accepts us – unconditionally, warts and all! It means being gentle and kind with ourselves as a 'work in progress'. 'Kindness to self' is about taking responsibility to care for ourselves. Our compassionate mind is never critical. It is conscious of our weaknesses, but its overriding qualities are of kindness and acceptance.

It's important to note that focusing on kindness can make us feel sad or vulnerable, because it can hook into a deep pain arising from the acknowledgement that no one has ever shown us kindness in our life. If this happens, we may need to use other 'warm' thoughts – of fun, kind humour, approval, praise or congratulation – to challenge self-critical thoughts for a while. However, it would be healthy and helpful to return to those harder thoughts at some point, in order to explore and understand why kindness makes us feel sad – perhaps with the help of a friend or counsellor. This exploration needs sensitivity and kindness: Chris likens it to opening a bottle of fizzy pop slowly, rather than allowing it to explode.

Addressing our negative thinking: The use of mindfulness

Trying to take every thought captive, challenging it and replacing it, or even listing 'good things' may, for some of us, be too exhausting. It is easy to feel a failure at such tasks, which in turn leads to more self-critical thoughts and deeper depression. So, another way of trying to address and manage depressive thoughts is to adopt a 'mindfulness' approach. The skill of mindfulness helps us to learn how to observe ourselves, our feelings and our thoughts in a detached way. Instead of talking to ourselves with little more than criticism or rebuke, we listen and respond in a 'mindful' way, *without* judgment but with compassion.

The psalms give us clear examples for turning our negative self-talk around using mindfulness:

Why are you downcast, O my soul?
    Why so disturbed within me?
Put your hope in God,
    for I will yet praise him,
    my Saviour and my God.

(Psa. 42:11)

The psalmist begins by talking to himself: 'Why are you downcast, O my soul?' In other words: 'Why are you feeling so depressed?' But he challenges his feelings, rather than allowing his self-talk to continue in a negative mode. In effect, he says: 'Self, listen for a moment, *I* will speak to *you*! Why are you so cast down? Why so distressed? Come on – put your hope in God!' In previous lines, he has reminded himself of all that God is and has done – 'These things I remember' – and finally he says 'I will yet praise him' – or, 'I will make it through, there will be an end to this, God is worthy of my praise.'

In Psalm 22:1–5, the process takes a little longer but the 'turnaround' is still there:

> My God, my God, why have you forsaken me?
>   Why are you so far from saving me,
>   so far from the words of my groaning?
> O my God, I cry out by day, but you do not answer,
>   by night, and am not silent.
>
> Yet you are enthroned as the Holy One;
>   you are the praise of Israel.
> In you our fathers put their trust...

The turnaround comes on the word 'yet', as the psalmist reminds himself who God is and what He has done, and that He can be trusted totally. This is the essence of helping ourselves to understand how to handle this hurting person within us: to not listen passively to him or allow him to drag us down, but to simply notice him at times, challenge him at other times, and be kind and compassionate, rather than condemning and angry. We are to be self-aware and to know how to handle ourselves –

however we are feeling. Mindfulness helps us to do that.

Mindfulness acknowledges and fully lives the present moment without labelling, analysing, judging, trying to understand, or 'trying *not* to think about it'. The frequency of any thought that we try *not* to think about may reduce for a short while, but will soon recur more frequently than before. Instead of disappearing, the thought we want *not* to think about becomes more central to our thinking and, consequently, even more likely to evoke a response. The following exercise illustrates the point:

- 'Place' a clear picture in your mind of a bright red tractor.
- Try hard *not* to think of it for one minute. (Time yourself.)
- Now try hard to think about that red tractor and – whatever other thoughts come into your mind – give it all the attention it needs, again for one minute.

When we try the red tractor exercise we will probably find that the more we try not to think of the red tractor the more we keep returning to it, whereas when we give ourselves permission to think about it, other thoughts crowd into our minds to compete, and we don't think about the red tractor as much. When we try *not* to think of something, we do so by creating a verbal rule: 'Don't think of "x"!' But this tends to evoke 'x' even more because we will remember what we are trying not to think of (ie the red tractor). So, the wearisome thought grows. Paradoxically, well-intentioned attempts to suppress or eliminate depressing thoughts, memories and emotions (x) often intensify the experiences associated with them.

Mindfulness tackles this tendency by engaging the mind in the here and now – the present moment. It asks us to attend to and observe the present moment without analysis and judgment. Mindfulness doesn't try to control depression. Instead, it helps us to feel and accept what we feel fully, without judgment, based on the assumption that most unwanted feelings and thoughts cannot be eliminated or controlled, but are to be accepted. We learn to step back and observe those thoughts, rather than become fused with them or controlled by them: '*I* am not my thoughts.' Mindfulness allows us to recognise our thoughts and feelings, but not be defined by them. For example, 'I am feeling anxious' means I have the feeling of being anxious at this moment, not necessarily that I am an anxious person.

The purpose of mindfulness is to learn how to distance ourselves from thoughts and feelings by observing them and giving them no evaluation. There is neither a right nor wrong way to be mindful: it simply involves trying to be a conscious observing self in the moment. If evaluations do occur, we observe them but neither believe nor disbelieve them. (If we do either, a battle will ensue!) Judging those thoughts as 'good' or 'bad' does not allow us to be mindful.

In practice, we can become 'mindful' by taking a series of steps:

1. Engage our mind in the here and now.
We don't resist feelings and thoughts, even when our mind wanders (or those thoughts will become stronger – remember the red tractor?)
Then we...

2. Observe and attend to our feelings and thoughts 'in the moment' without evaluating or judging them. In a sense, we give them a word or two on the doorstep, rather than inviting them in to the party!
Then we...

3. Describe what we observe in an objective way.

We learn to differentiate between observing self and experiencing self, and change the way we label our thoughts and feelings:

- 'I feel so anxious' becomes:
  'I am experiencing the feeling of anxiety.'
- 'I am stupid' becomes:
  'I am thinking that I am stupid.'
- 'I am depressed' becomes:
  'I am noticing that my body feels heavy, and my feelings are saying that I am worthless.'

4. If thoughts become too overwhelming, we can bring ourselves back to the present moment by becoming aware of our breathing rhythm, taking some slow deep breaths, and becoming aware of how our body feels. This distraction technique helps us to be grounded in the present, rather than letting our thoughts take us to the past or the future.

We can also help to 'defuse' our thoughts by changing the normal context in which they occur. We might do this by:

- Repeating the thought in a silly voice, slower or faster as if to master it, render it less powerful, or become familiar with it.
- Viewing our mind as something external: 'Well, that's just my mind worrying again!'
- Just noticing: 'I am just noticing that I am judging myself at the moment'.
- 'Buying' thoughts: 'I am buying the thought that I am hopeless, because I am depressed'.
- 'Seeing monsters on a bus': we can treat thoughts as if they are monsters on a bus we are driving! It's best to keep

moving, rather than trying to get them to leave, or do what they say!

- Dismissing the thought: 'It's just a thought!' And tell it promptly: 'Sit down and shut up!'
- Carrying it: write a negative thought on a slip of paper, and carry it as a metaphor: it signifies that we can carry thoughts without being controlled by them. Eventually we will find the 'thought' screwed up in a pocket, and throw it away.

David went to a counsellor with deep depression and the inability to live in the present moment. He always thought the worst, to the extent that he couldn't go out and enjoy a meal with his wife because he constantly thought his enjoyment would soon be over. Learning the practice of mindfulness enabled him to move forward. He was taught how to observe himself and be fully aware of thoughts and feelings in the present moment. When out for a meal with his wife he was encouraged to concentrate on how he experienced every mouthful of food, and to enjoy what he was eating, rather than anticipating that the evening would soon end. Practising mindfulness led to significant improvement, and in his last session David said: 'If only someone had shown me these skills years ago, I would have enjoyed life so much more.'

Changing our negative thinking: Cultivating an 'attitude of gratitude'

The common advice to 'count your blessings', so that your mood is lifted, is founded in fact. It really does help.

Research by Lyubomirsky et al (2005)[4] highlights the benefits of counting our blessings once a week. Emmons and McCullough (2003)[5] suggest finding five positive things to write about every week, for ten weeks, to see a positive improvement in mood.

In a similar vein, Luks (2001)[6] suggests that depressed people can motivate themselves by performing random acts of kindness. He found there was a 57 per cent increase in self-esteem, a 53 per cent increase in optimism, and a 53 per cent reduction in depression in those who performed kind acts. The greater the frequency of such acts, the more positive the outcome.

Activity

Try managing your negative thinking by engaging in one or more of the methods mentioned in this chapter (or encourage the person you are supporting to do so). If possible, keep a diary for at least a week or two to record your/their progress. Try not to give up too soon – change takes time.

Reflection

> Finally brothers, whatever is true, whatever is noble, whatever is right, whatever is pure, whatever is lovely, whatever is admirable – if anything is excellent or praiseworthy – think about such things... And the God of peace will be with you.
>
> (Phil. 4:8–9)

Spend some time considering how you might put Paul's encouraging words into practice.

Prayer

> May the mind of Christ, my Saviour,
> Live in me from day to day,
> By His love and power controlling
> All I do and say.
> May the Word of God dwell richly
> In my heart from hour to hour,
> So that all may see I triumph
> Only through His power.

From a hymn by Kate Barclay Wilkinson (1859–1928)

CHAPTER 6

Under the dark cloud – Depression and faith

We mentioned earlier just how difficult it often is for Christians to come to terms with being depressed. It is as if we feel that faith should exempt us from depressive episodes; that we should be 'above all that', or that if we have God – 'in him is no darkness at all' – the experience of spiritual, mental or emotional darkness should not be ours.

Yet Christians *do* suffer from depression – and often find that the burden of the illness itself is increased by the response of other Christians who judge, misunderstand or dismiss the experience. Consequently, a depressed Christian is often an isolated Christian, who finds it hard to be honest about their experience in the very place they should find acceptance, care and love: the church.

Sometimes it is pride, or ignorance of the reality of depression, that keeps sufferers in a silent place ('Real Christians don't get depressed'); it may be fear ('What will people say?') or shame ('I must be a bad person because I'm depressed'). Sometimes a church with a strong emphasis on certain hard-to-achieve Christian disciplines may trigger depression amongst members, as they feel they can never 'match up' or be 'acceptable'.

Annie attended an independent church for many years. There was much that Annie agreed with and enjoyed, but to her there seemed to be an over-emphasis on sanctification, on cleansing her life and changing her character to become more like Jesus. She said that it appeared all very sound and biblical, but in her spirit she felt there was something wrong: 'I began to feel I would never be cleansed enough to be accepted in heaven.' As a result she began to feel uncertain about her walk with Jesus, and she became depressed. It was only when she left the church that she realised the impact of the teaching she had absorbed. Eventually, she found a worshipping community who lived out God's loving acceptance, while still encouraging each other to become like Jesus through knowing His love and care. She is now feeling free, and knows that she is complete and accepted by God. Her depression has lifted.

Annie's situation was unusual: changing our church will rarely be the answer to depression. But Annie's experience shows how a lack of opportunity to accept our humanity and our weaknesses, in the heart of a loving church family, can only exacerbate the problem.

Christians, like everyone else, are weak and fallible human beings. We may be able to cope with one major stress or loss, but when other stressful events follow in quick succession our inner resources may be unable to cope with such an onslaught. We cannot adjust emotionally to what is going on, or find the resources we need, so we are likely to become depressed. It is as if the whole of our being is saying: 'Enough!'

So, how might that experience relate to our spirituality?

The spiritual impact of depression

Depression in Christians is rarely caused by our spiritual life, but depression will affect us spiritually. When our life events are difficult or traumatic and we are not firmly rooted in our sense of identity in Christ, we may become aware of how 'self' is dealing with the issues we face. This can happen when we see our faith journey as:

- A life which follows a message of present forgiveness, without future hope.
- An ethical and moral way of living, enjoining us to do good in this world. (Ethics and morality will not help us with emotional or mental difficulties.)
- A matter of aesthetic appeal: we see the gospel as something wonderful which helps us to feel better, but little more.
- An intellectual and philosophical theory with no application to our personal life.
- A theological doctrine: our heads are engaged, but our hearts are never touched.
- An emotional experience: if we base everything only on words we will dry up, but if we base everything only on feelings we will blow up! Our faith life needs substance and purpose, and must be anchored in reality.

Our faith journey may be affected by depression when our 'spiritual symptoms' include:

- An inability to pray.
- Difficulty (or unwillingness) in reading the Bible.
- A lack of joy in worship and fellowship.
- A sense of 'losing our faith' or not being able to make sense of it.

- Believing that we have fallen out of favour with God, and with other Christians.
- A lack of purpose or focus in service: doing the tasks we believe God has given us to do for Him and others.

All of us will experience each of those symptoms at some point. We also need to be reassured that experiencing any one or any combination is not necessarily a sign of depression: not making sense of our faith, for example, means that we are experiencing doubt. However, as we mentioned earlier, doubt – contrary to popular belief – is part of faith, not the opposite of faith. The opposite of faith is total certainty! Our faith life will ebb and flow in strength and enthusiasm, just like any other area of our life: stress, tiredness, lack of time and disordered priorities will all take their toll. To regain balance in our life, we may need to make time and space for whichever essential activities we have overlooked. But if we experience continuously more than one or two of those 'spiritual symptoms', our unhappiness may deepen.

We may have arrived at that unhappy place for a variety of reasons. Dr Martyn Lloyd-Jones has written that 'spiritual depression or unhappiness in the Christian life is very often due to our failure to realise the greatness of the Gospel'.[1] The completeness of the gospel requires engagement with the heart, the mind and the will, leading to personal wholeness. The gospel reveals that Jesus died so that we might become whole people, not merely that certain parts of us may be affected by the gospel and 'saved'. We are called not to be lop-sided Christians, but Christians who live with a balance between the mind, the heart and the will. We see this balance perfectly demonstrated in Jesus. The gospel encompasses and embraces the whole of life, the whole of history, and all of humanity in a complete and all-inclusive understanding of life; it is a holistic, 'whole-istic' gospel. It draws on, and pours into every detail of, our life – nothing of our self or experience is excluded from it. Failing to understand the totality of the gospel may prevent us from living out a full life of faith.

As Christians, we have been given the gift of the Holy Spirit, with His transforming power and comfort. We are taught to develop a view of life that is essentially different from the one we held before we came to faith. That view will not always offer us an easy life, or perfect understanding of all that befalls us, but it does offer us security in a close relationship with God – Father, Son and Holy Spirit.

Caution is needed here, however. In the 1970s, a popular bumper sticker asked: 'If you feel far from God, guess who's moved?'

It may certainly be that when our focus shifts from God to ourselves, when we allow sin to create a barrier in our relationship with Him, or when we choose deliberate disobedience to what we know is God's way for us to live, then it *is* us who has 'moved'. But in some circumstances, such a conviction only loads us with guilt – and usually false guilt.

When depression is reactive – for example as part of a grieving process – it is an entirely normal and necessary part of our emotional response (think of David grieving for Absalom: 2 Samuel 18:33). What is important is the path that depression takes. God can be found on that path, and especially in the darkness – indeed, He weeps with us. And He can lead us out of the darkness if we are willing to be found by Him. If God remains our focus, even when we can hardly find Him, we will not 'move'. We may have done nothing to cause our sense of separation. What we can be sure of is that whatever we feel, God is constant and faithful.

We are saved by the grace, mercy and unconditional love of God. That love does not lessen because of our depression. We must remind ourselves that depression is never a 'punishment' from God, or a sign of His love being taken away from us. Our relationship with God doesn't depend upon our being 'good' or 'perfect', but upon Him always being gracious. He loves us just as we are. There is, to paraphrase Philip Yancey in his book *What's so Amazing about Grace?*, nothing we can do to make God love us more, and equally, nothing we can do to make Him love us less. He just loves us – more than we can ever know.

God wants an intimate relationship with us, but that doesn't mean we always feel close to Him! The important thing is that God doesn't change His nature or position. He is constant and omnipresent. Whether we are aware of it or not, He offers unconditional love – and holds us in that love, however insecure we may feel. He offers us security, self-worth and significance: security in His eternal plan and providence, and in the Holy Spirit's comfort and power; self-worth in the knowledge that Jesus the Son valued us enough to die for us; and significance as children of God the Father.

It may be difficult to understand the 'whys' and 'wherefores' of the kind of depression that makes us feel far from God. The relationship between depression and faith is made of many strands, not easily separated. The best place to begin our search for understanding is with the God who loves and cares for us. As we have said, God designed us to be whole people, secure as His children, fulfilled by His love and filled with His Spirit. But He also knows our weaknesses. He knows 'how we are formed' (Psa. 103:14).

The Bible highlights the experience of depression – some of its greatest and most faithful personalities suffered in the grip of this condition – and the Bible offers real and practical help to the afflicted. We can draw comfort from their response to depression – and, more importantly, from God's response. Pablo Martinez writes '... these men and women were indeed spiritual giants but they were also flesh and blood, "of like passions and sufferings with us" (James 5:17, ASV). God in his mysterious sovereignty uses vessels of clay and not of gold.'[2]

How the Bible portrays depression

Elijah (1 Kings 19:1–18)

God has finally thundered His judgment against the evil King Ahab through His prophet Elijah, and He tells Elijah to flee away from the king's reach. Although God promises to provide sustenance and Elijah has given his all to God, he still considers that his mission has failed and he is left feeling rejected, fearful and isolated – all typical symptoms of depression. So Elijah prays that he might die: 'I have had enough Lord... Take my life; I am no better than my ancestors' (v4). He then does what those who suffer from depression so often do: he withdraws, and sleeps. He does the desert version of switching off the phone, locking the front door, and pulling the duvet over his head. He doesn't have the inner resources to withstand the onslaught of hopelessness and despair, and becomes deeply depressed. Events have become too much for Elijah, and he breaks down.

But later, in a powerful conversation with God, he is re-commissioned. God doesn't even mention Elijah's depression, but points forward to his new responsibility. It's not that God doesn't care, but that Elijah's depression is of no consequence to God's ends. He still believes in Elijah. It is clear that He still considers Elijah to be 'his man'. Elijah's story offers powerful encouragement to us when we believe God can no longer use us.

Moses (Numbers 11:14-35)

In the initial phase of his depression, Moses blames God for his struggle with a complaining people. His questions reveal his sense of despair. This heartfelt outpouring of complaint is a necessary part of his 'therapy' before God. Even Moses, 'more humble than anyone else on the face of the earth' (Num. 12:3), expresses his intense disappointment.

But notice that he doesn't complain about or against God – he just opens his heart in honesty. It is never wrong to tell God honestly how we feel. Moses' thinking is distorted by his emotional state. The 'burden' is too heavy, he says, and in verse 15 his depression, like Elijah's, culminates in thoughts of death. God's response gives us the perfect blueprint for helping those who are depressed.

First, God shows understanding. He does not censure Moses for his depression, but merely listens. Secondly, God arranges practical help by assigning a whole team of elders to help Moses with the people, while still leaving him in control. Thirdly, God offers encouragement for Moses' self-esteem (v17) in re-commissioning him. God does not remove the responsibility of leadership from Moses – but confirms him in it. Moses emerges a restored and newly confident leader, loved and valued by a God who cares for him.

Job (encapsulated by Job 30:26-31)

Job's story of depression is perhaps the hardest for us to take.

Here is a faithful man, brought to his knees by unjust disaster. It seems that God has allowed almost complete devastation of Job's blameless life (Job 1:1,12). He has lost everything.

But God's agenda cannot be taken at 'face-value'. He knows His 'servant Job' (1:8), and with Job's story God gives us a glimpse of how He sees our lives and the difficulties they contain. God sees us through a very different lens from our own. Job is allowed to ask 'Why?' over and over again as he pours out his heart in an effort to affirm his own humanity, before God finally answers. At the end of Job's period of great desolation and depression, God's reply sets Job's experience in a much broader context – that of his relationship with the creator of the universe. God does not give simple, easy answers to Job in the midst of his anguish. Instead, He gives something much more valuable. Michael Mayne writes: 'Job must learn that there are absolute limits to the extent of human understanding... that God does not give answers. Instead, he gives himself.'[3]

Martha and Mary (John 11:1–43)

The fact that God 'gives Himself' is poignantly evident in the story of Martha and Mary, and the raising from the dead of their brother Lazarus. At first, with Jesus absent as His friend is first taken ill and then dies, Martha and Mary must have asked many questions: 'Where is He? Why doesn't He do something?' – legitimate questions from a place of despair. When He does arrive, Jesus raises Lazarus to life, demonstrating His power over death and decay: but not before He has stood alongside Mary and Martha in their confusion, depression and grief, and wept with them (v35). Later, of course, He would demonstrate the ultimate response to death and darkness when He did indeed 'give Himself', to give new life not just to Lazarus, Martha and Mary, but to all of us.

The psalmists

The psalmists, King David included, offer us perhaps the most striking acceptance of the experience of depression. They speak of 'whys' and 'wheres'; of darkness and depth; pits and blindness – all metaphors for depression. Psalms 13, 22, 42 and 88, amongst others, frame the experience for us and offer us words we cannot find for ourselves, to express our pain to God. These psalms are raw and honest, and they never pull punches. Walter Brueggemann writes: 'These psalms make the important connection; everything must be brought to speech, and everything brought to speech must be addressed to God, who is the final reference for all of life.'[4] The psalmists address their heart to God through the psalms in words which are as contemporary, relevant, fresh and honest as the day they were written.

These scriptures, together with the stories of Abraham, Jeremiah, Jonah, Jacob and numerous others, illustrate God's response to depression.

What can we conclude? That darkness, depression and despair are common – and even legitimate – spiritual experiences. The prophet Isaiah certainly thought so:

> Who among you fears the LORD
>   and obeys the word of his servant?
> Let him who walks in the dark,
>   who has no light,
> trust in the name of the LORD
>   and rely on his God.

(Isa. 50:10)

If God's response to the depression of the faithful, as illustrated in the Bible, is primarily practical and motivating, so should ours be.

A practical response

Knowing that God understands the place we are in, being honest before Him, and taking comfort from the biblical perspective on depression, we can develop a response to help us through depression. Our practical and personal response may include these strategies:

1. Pray

Prayer needs no words: sighs, tears and even silence are accepted by God as prayer. And we can pray even if we can't 'feel' God. He is still there. If we open our heart to Him in a dark place, He will give us the light we need to find our way out. There may be just a match-head of light to begin with, but it will grow.

2. Hang on to what we know is true

Depression pulls us away from the things in life that we value. We may need to rediscover our worth in God's sight, going back to the very roots of our faith. We can rebuild it – and our strength with it. We may slowly rediscover a tentative commitment to living (for God) in which we are willing to experience our feelings and thoughts, both wanted and unwanted, and do what is valuable and life-affirming. (See the story about Sophie on page 123.) Meditating on a few simple, well-loved Bible verses, prose or poetry, music or art, that meant a lot to us when we were 'in the light', may help.

3. Remember there are no 'oughts'

God does not insist that we go to church, attend a homegroup, read our Bible three times a day, pray for half an hour, or smile our 'Christian smile'. God just wants a relationship with us – however we are able to shape it. We might be helped by looking for God in new and different places: through the natural world or beautiful music; in books, during walks, or when talking and reminiscing with loved ones. So often we make our God too small by only expecting to find Him in the usual places: in the formalities of organised worship, or the structures of a church organisation. But God is beyond our imagination, and will constantly reveal Himself to us in new and inviting ways – if we look beyond the ordinary, and free ourselves from the familiar and expected.

4. Ask for the support, commitment and prayer of a trusted friend, counsellor or pastor

This *may* begin with our exploring together those areas of our life in which we need to seek – and accept – God's forgiveness. Later we may ask for a regular time to pray together and share thoughts and feelings before God; or just to spend time together over a coffee; shopping; enjoying the countryside; or sharing the preparation and enjoyment of a meal. It may help to keep a faith journal, and share parts of it with our friend in order to pray honestly.

5. Being kind to oneself

We may need encouragement to rest, sleep, eat well, laugh, and enjoy life. We must give ourselves time and space to find the God who is searching for our hearts more than we are searching for His: He will be found, if we seek Him.

When Sophie was depressed, she found herself 'hanging onto faith by my fingernails'. She found it helpful to go back to the very basics of her faith. She started by remembering how she came to faith in the first place. Then she began to consider what she felt she could believe. This led her to an exploration of Jesus, the man, through reading the Gospels. To her astonishment, she found herself falling in love with Him all over again: recognising Him as both an amazing human being and as the unique Son of God. Sophie realised that much of what she was rejecting in the midst of depression was simply a shaky formalised structure for a life of faith: one that was founded on her own assumptions and misunderstanding. Meeting God again meant that she met Him on His terms, not her own – it was as if He was excitedly introducing Himself! She now says that her faith was positively strengthened – and energised – by her experience of depression.

When depression 'isn't': Recognising 'The Dark Night of the Soul'

It is sometimes difficult to distinguish between depression which drains our spiritual lives, and what St John of the Cross referred to as 'The Dark Night of the Soul' – also described by an unknown author as 'The Cloud of Unknowing'. But this is an important distinction, and one which is upheld by many. 'The Dark Night of the Soul' is a time when God is referred to as *'Deus Absconditus'* – the God who is hidden.

Sometimes we do everything 'right': we are sure we have a sound understanding of faith and of God; we pray, we worship, and we serve as usual; yet we seem to know nothing but silence from God – a silence that may plunge us into darkness. We examine our hearts to find the reason for such silence, but find nothing. It feels, says George Buttrick, as if we are 'beating on heaven's door with bruised knuckles in the dark'.[5] This experience can last for days, weeks, months – perhaps years. Even Jesus after His arrest, in Gethsemane and on the cross, experienced the silence, darkness and apparent withdrawal of God the Father: 'My God, my God, why have you forsaken me?' (Mark 15:34).

Richard Foster writes that 'God is always present with us – we know that theologically – but there are times when he withdraws our consciousness of his presence... here we experience real spiritual desolation... nothing helps.' Foster writes that the biblical metaphor for such times is the desert or wilderness – dry, barren and parched; a place of wandering. He continues: 'These experiences of abandonment and desertion have come and will come to us all.'[6]

Because both spiritual dark nights and depression can include feelings of hopelessness and emptiness, affecting a person's thoughts, motivation and confidence, a distinction between the two experiences will be helpful. Gerald May, a psychiatrist and spiritual director, offers some guidelines. He says that 'dark night' experiences are not usually associated with loss of effectiveness at work or in general day-to-day functioning – often much to the surprise of the 'sufferer'. Those who have previously suffered depression may especially notice this distinction. The individual's sense of humour is usually retained – if anything it is enhanced following a 'dark night' – as is compassion for others; and the sufferer is far less self-absorbed. Rather, there is an unexplained yet very real sense of the 'rightness' of the experience, however difficult it may be; however bewildering or confusing. This is in contrast, of course, to the experience of someone suffering from depression, for whom everything seems 'wrong'. A person suffering a 'dark night' does not seem to be pleading for help – as does a clinically depressed person – and although the former may seek meaning, they do not seek escape. Gerald May concludes: 'very subtly, yet perhaps most importantly, one does not generally feel frustrated, resentful or annoyed in the presence of a person undergoing a dark night experience... one is much more likely to feel graced and consoled'.[7]

God may lead us into a 'dark night' for a season in order for us to discover that faith is greater than the light we long for to lighten our darkness; in order to bid us re-assess our relationship with Him; to meet Him afresh; or to consider the pace or commitment of our walk with Him. He may be challenging our view of His personhood, and asking us to grow. Canon Gordon Jeffs believes the recognition that our God is too small is one of the major causes of the 'dark night' and of God's apparent absence. He concludes: 'Painful though this may be, and long as it may last, it is nevertheless to do with growth. We shall remain in the darkness of love and longing until in God's own good time we perceive a glimmer of light... at the end of a tunnel, and gradually a new and more adequate image of God begins to form.'[8]

St John of the Cross, who first wrote about the 'Dark Night of the Soul' centuries ago, reassures those living in darkness: 'It is when you understand him [God] less clearly that you are coming closer to him... you do well at all times whether life, or faith, is smooth or hard, you do well to hold God as hidden, and so cry out to him, "Where have you hidden?"' (Canticle 112 passim).

Frederick Buechner writes that to be commanded to love God in the wilderness is like being commanded to be well when we are sick, or to run when we are lame: 'But this is the first and great commandment nonetheless. Even in the wilderness – especially in the wilderness – you shall love him.'[9] Because He first loved us.

In conclusion

The experience of depression need not be all negative. Many depressed people will say that their experience has given them a fresh understanding of their own humanity and of their God; depression has tested and strengthened their faith, increased their empathy, and deepened their wisdom. A significant minority would not want to revisit their time of depression, but look back on it with gratitude. They may still have unanswered questions, but they trust that God holds – and eternity will reveal – the answers. And, perhaps surprisingly, that is often enough.

Felicity has known deep experiences both of depression, and of the 'dark night', and is able to see the distinction. She believes that while God allowed the depression – and stood with her in those times – He led her into the 'desert' and the 'dark night'. In retrospect, she says that all of these dark and bewildering times have borne fruit in her life. 'God's relationship with us is one of mystery,' she says, 'but I would not have a God with whom my relationship was not a mystery – however hard. Because in that mystery hides the greatest love.'

Activity

Think of the dark experience of a Bible character, or a dark experience of your own. How does the Bible explain those experiences, and the 'symptoms' they produce?

Reflection

Read the following poem:

> I used to think there was a point in even the
> greatest suffering:
> A glimmer of hope; some small triumph;
> A victory cry running through the veins of pain.
> But there is none.
> There is no point but the stabbing point that wounds.
> There is only God.
> Yet even He hides Himself in dark draperies.
> He waits concealed behind walls of silence or lurks
> in the shadows of hopelessness, so that I cannot
> recognise Him.
>> From Wendy Bray, *Prayer to a Hidden God*[10]

Reflect on these words for a few moments. Do you find them difficult? Upsetting? What would you want to say to the writer? Might these words help you to express your heart to God in dark times?

Prayer

My God, My God why have you forsaken me?
Why are you so far from saving me,
so far from the words of my groaning?
O my God, I cry out by day, but you do not answer,
by night and am not silent.

Yet you are enthroned as the Holy One;
you are the praise of Israel.
In you our fathers put their trust;
they trusted and you delivered them.
They cried to you and were saved;
in you they trusted and were not disappointed.

(Psa. 22:1–5)

When the light is dimmed – or disappears altogether, plunging us into darkness – we may yet discover that there is something brighter, surer and more eternal than the light. And that is God's love.

Appendix 1

How depressed am I?

RATING MY MOOD

Below are some possible symptoms of depression.

Describe how you feel at the moment by placing an x at the appropriate point on the line.

Example:

I am very hungry   I am very full

————————————X————————————————

I feel really sad   I feel fine and not unhappy

I feel anxious and panicky   I don't feel particularly anxious

I feel very guilty all the time   I don't feel guilty at all

I feel weepy and unusually   I feel emotionally
emotional   well-balanced

I have no energy   I have plenty of energy

I have no motivation   My motivation is as usual

My thoughts are very negative   My thoughts are balanced

I don't enjoy doing anything any more	I enjoy myself as usual
I have difficulty in making decisions	I can make decisions
I have constant self-critical thoughts	I have a balanced view of myself
I have difficulty getting to sleep/I wake early	I sleep normally
My eating habits have changed	My appetite is normal
I feel lethargic and much less active than usual	I am as active as normal
I feel hopeless about the future	I am optimistic about the future
I have lost my faith	My faith is strong

You could discuss what this exercise has shown you with your friend/carer/counsellor.

Appendix 2

Daily thought diary

Use this diary – or model your own on it – to record your thoughts, as suggested to 'Sue' in Chapter 5.

Thought	Evidence	Alternative, balanced thought

Further reading

Books offering a practical framework for understanding depression:

Paul Gilbert, *Overcoming Depression: A Self-Help Guide using Cognitive Behavioural Techniques* (London: Constable and Robinson, 2000)

Dr John Lockley, *A Practical Workbook for the Depressed Christian* (Milton Keynes: Authentic, 2002)

Dorothy Rowe, *Depression – The Way Out of Your Prison,* 3rd edition (Abingdon: Routledge, 2003)

Kirk D. Strosahl, Patricia J. Robinson, *The Mindfulness and Acceptance Workbook for Depression* (Oakland, CA: New Harbinger Publications, 2008)

Books exploring a personal experience of depression from a Christian perspective:

Sue Atkinson, *Climbing Out of Depression*, 2nd edition (Oxford: Lion Publishing, 2005)

Dr Martyn Lloyd-Jones, *Spiritual Depression* (Grand Rapids, MI: Eerdmans, 1965)

Hazel Rolston, *Beyond the Edge: One Woman's Journey out of Post-Natal Depression and Anxiety* (Westmont, IL: IVP, 2008)

Veronica Zundel, *'Crying for the Light': Bible Readings and Reflections for Living with Depression* (Abingdon: Bible Reading Fellowship, 2008)

Books which, though not focused on depression, contain valuable chapters or sections on the experience of depression:

Ronald Dunn, *When Heaven is Silent* (Nashville, TN: Nelson Word, 1994)

Steve Griffiths, *God of the Valley: a Journey through Grief* (Abingdon: Bible Reading Fellowship, 2003)

Pablo Martinez, *A Thorn in the Flesh: Finding Strength and Hope Amid Suffering* (Westmont, IL: IVP, 2007)

Philip Yancey, *Disappointment with God* (Grand Rapids, MI: Zondervan, 1988)

Helpful information

Childline – 0800 1111

Saneline – 0300 304 7000

Samaritans – 116 123, or find your local number; samaritans.org

lift-depression.com

youngminds.org.uk – Provides excellent information and resources for supporting young people with mental health problems, including depression.

cwmt.org.uk – The Charlie Waller Memorial Trust, offering support for sufferers of depression and their families.

time-to-change.org.uk – Campaigns for new approaches to mental health issues.

who.int/news-room/fact-sheets/detail/depression

Endnotes

Introduction
1. Jo Revill, *The Observer*, Sunday 24 February 2008

Chapter 1
1. For more on this idea of 'the black dog', see the World Health Organization's video: 'I had a black dog, his name was depression', youtube.com/watch?v=XiCrniLQGYc [Accessed September 2019]

2. Sue Chance, 1996 – healthieryou.com/exclusive/chancethe0196.html

3. William Styron, *'Darkness Visible': A Memoir of Madness* (New York: Random House, 1990), p7

4. Adapted from George Brown and Tirril Harris, *Social Origins of Depression* (London: Tavistock, 1978)

5. Statistics taken from: Mind, 'How common are mental health problems?', mind.org.uk [Accessed September 2019] And The British Medical Journal, 'NHS prescribed record number of antidepressants last year', bmj.com [Accessed September 2019]

6. John White, *The Masks of Melancholy* (Downers Grove: IVP, 1982), p77

7. Adapted, *Social Origins of Depression* op. cit.

8. D.L. Rosenhan and M.E.P. Seligman, *Abnormal Psychology*, 3rd edition (New York: W.W. Norton and Company, 1995), p351

9. Grace Ketterman, *Depression Hits Every Family* (Nashville, TN: Oliver Nelson, 1988), pp16–19

10. Adapted from *The Diagnostic and Statistical Manual of Mental Disorders*, 4th edition (Primary Care Version, p39. [DSM-IV-PC], 1994/2000. Currently under revision)

11. Rowan Williams, *Tokens of Trust* (Norwich: Canterbury Press, 2007), p155

12. Henry Vaughan, seventeenth-century poet

Chapter 2
1. *The Times*, Monday 5 November 2007

2. P. Branney and A. White, *Big Boys Don't Cry: Depression and Men: Advances in Psychiatric Treatment* (in press)

3. S. Brownhill, K. Wilhelm, L. Barclay, V. Schmied, ' *"Big Build": Hidden Depression in Men'*, Australian and New Zealand Journal of Psychiatry, 2005, 39, pp921–31

4. Dr Paul Keedwell, *How Sadness Survived* (Abindon: Radcliffe Publishing Ltd, 2008), quoted in Jo Revill, *The Observer*, 24 February 2008

5. Adapted from Myra Chave-Jones, *Coping with Depression* (Lion Hudson, 1981)

6. Oliver James elaborates on this in *The Selfish Capitalist: the Origins of Affluenza* (London: Vermillion, 2008)

Chapter 3
1. Chris Ledger and Wendy Bray, Insight into Perfectionism (Farnham: CWR, 2009)

2. C.G. Jung, *'Psychotherapy', Collected Works*, trans. R.F.C. Hull (London: Routledge & Kegan Paul, 1960), p310

3. Dorothy Rowe, *Depression* (London: Routledge, 2003), p150

4. *Collins English Dictionary* (London: William Collins Sons & Co Ltd, 1976)

5. Wendy Bray and Diana Priest, Insight into Bereavement (Farnham: CWR, 2006)

6. Myra Chave-Jones, op. cit.
7. Hazel Rolston, *Beyond the Edge* (Nottingham: IVP, 2008), p.92.
8. Ibid.
9. Adapted from Dr John Lockley, *A Practical Workbook for the Depressed Christian* (Milton Keynes: Authentic, 2002), p.180.

Chapter 4
1. *Who Do You Think You Are?*, BBC1, Monday 16 February 2008.

Chapter 5
1. Dr Caroline Leaf, *Who Switched Off My Brain?* (Rivonia, South Africa: Pty Ltd, 2008).
2. Francis Frangipane, *The Three Battlegrounds* (Chichester: New Wine Press, 1994), p.28.
3. Paul Gilbert, *The Compassionate Mind* (London: Constable and Robinson, 2009).
4. S. Lyubomirsky, K. Sheldon and D. Schkade, 'Pursuing Happiness and the Architecture of Sustainable Change', *Review of Psychology*, 2005 9(2), pp.111–31.
5. R.A. Emmons and M.E. McCullough, 'Counting Blessings Versus Burdens; An Experimental Investigation of Gratitude and Subject Wellbeing in Daily Life', Journal Personal Social Psychology 84(2), pp.377–89, 2003.
6. Dr Allan Luks, *Health Benefits of Altruism* (The Random Acts of Kindness Foundation, 2001).

Chapter 6
1. Dr Martyn Lloyd-Jones, *Spiritual Depression* (Grand Rapids, MI: Eerdmans, 1965).
2. Pablo Martinez, *A Thorn in the Flesh* (Nottingham: IVP, 2007), p.49.
3. Michael Mayne, *Love, Pray, Remember* (London: Darton, Longman and Todd, 1998), p.49.
4. Walter Brueggemann, *The Message of the Psalms* (Minneapolis, MN: Augsberg, 1984), p.52.
5. George Arthur Buttrick, *Prayer* (New York: Abingdon Cokesbury, 1942), p.263.
6. Richard Foster, *Prayer: Finding the Heart's True Home* (London: Hodder and Stoughton, 1992), p.18.
7. Gerald May, Care of the Mind, Care of the Spirit; a Psychiatrist explores Spiritual Direction (New York: HarperCollins, 1992), pp.109–10, in Sue Pickering, Spiritual Direction (Norwich: Canterbury Press, 2008), p.184.
8. Gordon Jeffs, *Spiritual Direction for Every Christian* (London: SPCK, 2007), p.49.
9. Frederick Buechner quoted in Philip Yancey, *Disappointment with God* (Grand Rapids, MI: Bondservant, 1988), p.208.
10. Wendy Bray, *Prayers for Living* (Farnham: CWR, 2009), p.65.

Insight series

Handling issues that are often feared, ignored or misunderstood.

Courses

CWR's Insight courses draw on real-life case studies, biblical examples and counselling practices to offer insight on important topics, including depression, anxiety, stress, anger and self-acceptance. These courses have been developed by CWR's experienced tutors in response to the great need to help people understand and work through key issues.

These invaluable teaching days are designed both for those who would like to come for their own benefit and for those who seek to support or understand people facing particular issues.

To find out more and to book, visit **cwr.org.uk/courses** or call 01252 784719

Books

CWR's Insight books give biblical and professional insight into some of the key issues that many people face today but are often feared, ignored or misunderstood. Covering a range of topics including anxiety, stress, bereavement and eating disorders, these books are suitable for both those facing the issues involved, as well as those supporting others. Each book includes case studies and practical insights.

Insight into Addiction
ISBN: 978-1-85345-661-9

Insight into Eating Disorders
ISBN: 978-1-85345-791-3

Insight into Anxiety
ISBN: 978-1-85345-662-6

Insight into Self-Esteem
ISBN: 978-1-85345-663-3

Insight into Bereavement
ISBN: 978-1-78259-233-4

Insight into Self-Harm
ISBN: 978-1-85345-960-3

Insight into Dementia
ISBN: 978-1-78259-121-4

Insight into Shame
ISBN: 978-1-78259-933-3

 ALSO AVAILABLE AS EBOOK/KINDLE

For a complete list of all titles available in this series, visit
cwr.org.uk/insight
Available online or from Christian bookshops.

LET'S TALK...

WHEN WAS THE LAST TIME YOU HAD AN HONEST CONVERSATION?

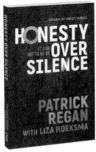 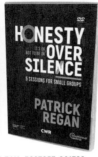

ISBN: 978-1-78259-833-6 EAN: 5027957-001732

Patrick Regan OBE is the CEO of Kintsugi Hope, and the founder of the urban youth work charity XLP.

Honesty Over Silence seeks to break the stigma around mental health and encourage open conversations that bring both understanding and hope. Powerful true stories from Patrick Regan and others about some of life's hardest challenges show how the strength in sharing honestly helps us to grow into the people God created us to be.

Based on the book, the five-session DVD includes interviews and discussion starters, making it ideal for use in small groups.

'It's going to provoke ten thousand honest conversations, helping to bring healing, hope and understanding to many who currently suffer in silence' – **Pete Greig**, founder of 24-7 Prayer

cwr.org.uk/HOS
Available online or from Christian bookshops.

Courses and seminars

Waverley Abbey College

Publishing and media

Conference facilities

Transforming lives

CWR's vision is to enable people to experience personal transformation through applying God's Word to their lives and relationships.
Our Bible-based training and resources help people around the world to:

- Grow in their walk with God
- Understand and apply Scripture to their lives
- Resource themselves and their church
- Develop pastoral care and counselling skills
- Train for leadership
- Strengthen relationships, marriage and family life and much more.

Our insightful writers provide daily Bible reading notes and other resources for all ages, and our experienced course designers and presenters have gained an international reputation for excellence and effectiveness.

CWR's Training and Conference Centre in Surrey, England, provides excellent facilities in idyllic settings - ideal for both learning and spiritual refreshment.

CWR Applying God's Word to everyday life and relationships

CWR, Waverley Abbey House,
Waverley Lane, Farnham,
Surrey GU9 8EP, UK

Telephone: +44 (0)1252 784700
Email: info@cwr.org.uk
Website: cwr.org.uk

Registered Charity No. 294387
Company Registration No. 1990308